wake up
MOTHER

wake up
MOTHER

STORIES AND WISDOM
SHARED BY MOTHERS

Curated by Sarah Lloyd
Held by the Unbound Press

ISBN 978-1-913590-83-3 Paperback
ISBN 978-1-913590-84-0 Ebook

The Unbound Press
www.theunboundpress.com

Hey unbound one!

Welcome to this magical book brought to you by The Unbound Press.

At The Unbound Press we believe that when women write freely from the fullest expression of who they are, it can't help but activate a feeling of deep connection and transformation in others. When we come together, we become more and we're changing the world, one book at a time!

This book has been carefully crafted by both the author and publisher with the intention of inspiring you to move ever more deeply into who you truly are.

We hope that this book helps you to connect with your Unbound Self and that you feel called to pass it on to others who want to live a more fully expressed life.

With much love,
Nicola Humber

Founder of The Unbound Press
www.theunboundpress.com

CONTENTS

PART 3 – HOW CAN WE REFRAME THE MOTHER?

213

MOTHER

Noun.

A Goddess on Earth.

A female figure of authority. A Creatrix.

The holder of the hearth, weaver of deep connection and one who tends to the inner wisdom and knowing.

A soothsayer who births, illuminates, protects and nurtures.

WHO THIS BOOK IS FOR...

This book has been written for those women who are firmly rocking their 'Mother' energy... for those women who have felt lost, alone, unsupported, dimmed, squashed, uncomfortable, unable to speak truth for fear of it highlighting the shadows.

It is for the Mothers, Sisters, Witches, Bitches, Whores and Good Girls.

It is for the Mothers of children, furry friends, businesses and creative projects.

The Mother Energy is the space we occupy between our Maidenhood* and our Crone**.

*Maidenhood – roughly speaking our teens and twenties – menarche – when we begin to move into our cycles/periods.

**Crone – when women hit their menopause and embrace their wisdom.

**Menarche – Menarche is the first menstrual cycle, or first menstrual bleeding, in female humans. From both social and medical perspectives, it is often considered the central event of female puberty, as it signals the possibility of fertility.

Mother is when we are most fertile physically. It is when we begin to nurture, guide and support those around us. It is our creative blooming, the ripening fruit, our period of birthing ideas, businesses, and babies.

It is also the time we are asked to quietly shoulder a lot.

Societal pressures, conditioning from authorities, media exposure and emotional immaturity are all designed to keep us forever in our girlhood and in our maidenhood.

The never-ending quest to stay young, look young, but still be successful – the cook in the kitchen and the whore in the bedroom. A construct designed to suit the patriarchy.

Add to that the pressure of procreation, biological clocks ticking, and being expected to carry on regardless. Our playground wounds playing out in adult life. Our inability to feel able to Mother ourselves for fear of being selfish. Emotionally immature women growing up alongside their children.

Taboos around the reality of childbirth, menarche, menstruation, perimenopause and menopause. Orgasms, leaky nipples, and female ejaculation. The reality is that babies are not just for Christmas.

Businesses, children and creative projects take a village to raise. It is in Mother Energy we find our communities, our village and ultimately our sanity.

The opportunity to face and embrace our shadows with no judgment.

It is within these shadows we find ourselves.

The parts of us, unseen or in the darkness. Those parts are hidden from the world and even in some cases yourself.

This book is like that bloody big search light looking over the ocean, shining a light on the unseen, the unspoken... wrapped up in a big cosy blanket of love.

Our intention with this book is to invite you to get comfortable and feel the energy of each of us as we share our stories.

Imagine if you will, us all sitting around a huge campfire, or a beautiful table in a classy wine bar; wherever you feel most at ease in receiving it.

Truly relax into the receiving energy.

Take those deep nourishing breaths that connect us to the Earth, to ourselves.... feel the oxygen buzzing around your body, permeating every cell.

And remember....

You are not alone.

Receive.

You are never alone.

Receive.

You are enough. Just as you are.

Receive.

And so it is, Dear One.

HOW TO CONNECT
WITH THIS BOOK

This book is a little like a sandwich – full of delicious yumminess. You can either read it cover to cover, flick through to see what wisdom or story wishes to make itself known to you, or you can dip into the parts that interest you the most.

Part One asks the question *What Does Mother Mean to You?*

It is here we dive into what that looks like for some of the contributors to this book, peppered with insight and research from other sources.

Part Two shares the wonderful and very varied stories about the Mother.

We have contributions from women who have birthed businesses, children and those who have not. Those at the beginning of their journey, and those more seasoned on the path. The beauty is there is something for every Mother.

Part Three is a shared opportunity to ask the question, how could we do things differently?

Our contributors once again weigh in and share their insights and advice. Many of the contributors have created businesses to support their own journey into Mother; so there is a shit tonne of resources you can access if you feel called to.

We love that you have landed here and trust that whatever medicine you need, you will receive it.

Huge love to you.

POETRY SHARED
BY OUR AUTHORS

An Ode to Mama

Be in the moment Mama
Slow down your pace
Be in the moment Mama
Feel the sun upon your face
Be in the Moment Mama
Fill up your cup
Sit there quietly and soak it all up.

Wipe your tears Mama
Let your feelings flow
You are no good to anyone when you are feeling low
Take the time Mama, to feel it all
The World will wait, and nothing will fall.

Take heart Mama
Know you are loved so much
It may not feel like it sometimes Mama
But you can feel it in their touch.

Lean in Mama
Find your quiet supportive space
Where there is no judgment, no frowns upon their face
Mama I see you quietly in the wings
Isn't it time you stepped up to sing?

Be gentle on yourself Mama
We are all you, and the stories that we share
Make each day easier to bear
We love you Mama we may not say it all the time
But know this Mama, I am so glad you are mine.

By Sarah Lloyd

A First Love

This is the hour they steal the moon.

Somewhere between midnight and morn,
she's drenched in moonshine, herself newborn.
Words hover in the ether betwixt two zones.
He wakes; a new dawn, hearts on loan.

Behind closed eyes, moments flash
Awakening nostalgia, the soft edges clash.
Memorable scents, memories too – long gone happenings
behind a rose-coloured hue.

It's the eyes – the eyes dazzle like a tempest of blue.
The intensity, held by the first gaze of love;
stars envelope the dark and become witnesses above.

Absorbing such richness feelings slowly creep, like a
weed knotting a whisper of emotion so deep.
Right here in this hour, the moon stolen again,
a realm of acceptance, heart bruises and pain.
Collision, connection, a thread from both,
entwined so delicately like an unspoken oath.

By Aimee Strongman

Arisen

From the tight pleats of our cloaked hearts
And the kindred depths
of our collective womb,
She awakens.

At first, wavering tendrils of green –
The tiniest, brazen shoots –
Begin to fur our energy,
And we choose
This time
Not to shave them away.
There is a subtle shift,
An opening––
A pregnant awe,
As we pass through the portal
Of a new awareness.
There is a tingling,
A memory bubbling up
Through sinews and cells
And synapses –
Electrifying and expanding
Our sensitivity to what IS
and *why*...
...And there is a mis-step:
Grief, guilt, disbelief, *rage*
Now rumbling up as if
From her very molten core;
Sobbing openly
For the miscarriage of justice
And her long, wrongful incarceration.

These sweet tendrils caress
and gently weave their way
Into the cave of our hearts;
Greening dark,
Breathing light,
Replenishing, renewing, remembering...
And suddenly we gasp –
A drowning life force breaking the surface,
An ancestral rebirth –
Flooding every particle of being
With deep nourishment
And love.

And we breathe anew.
Shedding our cloaks,
Spreading wide our wings,
Scrunching the earth between our toes –
Re-sensitising,
Reconnecting.
This sweet green web of wonder
Now filling our wombs:
Healing, cleansing, releasing
And – Oh!
She is there.
Her womb is our own,
Resplendent in roses
Abound, rising –
Goddess Mama,
We have arisen!

By Zoë Foster

Mamahood

Never knew you could feel so weak and so strong,
Both nights and days often seem far too long.
On cloud nine gazing at their sweet face,
Worn out and weary from the relentless pace.
Your body no longer somebody you know,
Marks of a Mama, unmistakable glow.

There is cultural pressure to bounce back to before,
As your evolving unfolds with a new YOU to explore.
Your arms are the haven where your babe is content
You are the safe space of pure nourishment.
Guilt, rage and worry weave through the daze,
Your heart is full of love, navigating each phase.

Believe in yourself Mama, their soul chose you
To guide them through life as only you can do.
It's joyful and hard, and there's regular drama
But there is nothing on earth quite like being a Mama

Dulcie Batt

Dear Mother Earth

They talk about you doing things wrong and being out of order

Your flowers are blooming too late, your patterns are changing

Yet I trust you

They talk about you being too hot here and too cold there

Yet I trust you

They talk about you melting, rising, vanishing

Yet I trust you

They talk of you like you're a victim and unintelligent

But they are wrong

I trust you
I trust your wisdom
I trust your intelligence
I trust you
I trust your seasons and your changing
I know you are not broken
Forever yours

By Kathy Bell

SYMBOLS

Symbols referring to different aspects of womanhood, specifically the Mother, have been in use since ancient times. These symbols carry deep and fascinating significance.

We wanted to share a few that may resonate as we journey together.

(Source - Symbolsage.com)

Triskele

The Celtic symbol for Mother. The symbol has three interlocking spirals, which come from a shared centre.

The triple spiral symbol characterises the three phases of womanhood which are Maiden, Mother and Crone.

The triple spiral represents many of life's trios.

It can depict the three trimesters of human pregnancy: life, death and rebirth; Father, Mother and Child.

In some communities it signifies past, present and future.

Triple Goddess

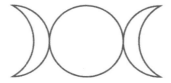

The Triple Goddess sign is familiar to Wiccans and Pagans.

The figure consists of a full moon sandwiched between a waning crescent moon on the right, and the waxing crescent on the left. It is a trinity of three deities united to one Mother figure.

Sometimes this sign is referred to as the **Mother Goddess**.

Each stage of the moon which makes up the Triple Goddess symbol correlates with stages of life as a woman.

The full moon characterises the woman as a caring Mother, while the two crescent-shaped moons on either side stand for the Crone (crown) and Maiden.

Some of the Goddesses characterised by this symbol are Demeter, Kore and Hecate.

The Maiden (crescent moon): Maiden embodies new beginnings, purity, pleasure, creation and naivety. If you focus on the maiden you enhance your spiritual, creative and sensual vigour.

The Mother (full moon): The Mother denotes responsibility, love, fertility, nourishment, patience and gratitude. Some cultures also argue she also represents self-care and control.

The Crone (fading moon): Just like the fading moon, Crone stands for endings, death, acceptance and wisdom. With every beginning there is an end. The Crone implores you to accept there will be no births and fresh beginnings where there are no death and endings.

The Triple Goddess also stands for the life cycles, namely life, birth and death.

It also connects with females, womanhood and the Divine Feminine.

Circle

As simple as the circle looks, it is an important symbol with deep implications. To Motherhood, it symbolises fertility.

This meaning arises from the perception of the rounded belly during pregnancy, the female chest and navel.

All these have circular shapes and play an important role in bringing about life and nurturing it.

The circle has no beginning or end, which perfectly depicts the infinite life cycle of birth, death, and rebirth.

It represents family ties and closeness. All wrapped up in the warm and caring embrace of a Mother.

Turtle

Common to North American culture, the Turtle is the oldest symbol depicting Motherhood.

There are ancient stories of how the turtle saved humanity from a great flood.

The turtle is also the symbol for Mother Earth.

Just as the turtle carries its house on its back, so does Mother Earth carry humanity's weight.

The turtle also produces many hatchlings at a go, for this reason it rightly symbolises fertility and the continuity of life.

Turtles have thirteen segments on their underbellies. They represent the thirteen lunar cycles of the moon and as we know this is often associated with feminine energy and vibrancy.

Furthermore, turtles have twenty-eight marks on them, these represent the 28 days of a woman's cycle.

The Seed of Life – Mary as the Triple Goddess

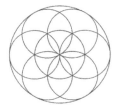

The Seed of Life is a **universal symbol of creation.**

The name of this pattern instantly offers insight into its deeper meaning and purpose. Found at the heart of an ancient symbol called the Flower of Life, there is an entire cosmology of consciousness encoded into this singular geometric seed.

In the Gospels, Mary Magdalene is a reworking of Isis the Triple Goddess. Her aspects are Bride, Mother, and Grandmother – wisdom keeper, and guardian of the natural world.

Mary as Mother: *"The Hebrew name Miriam (Mary) can be translated in various ways, but the letters taken as Hebrew ciphers mean; the flow of creative mutable power, containing as principles, the seeds of absolute life; Creative Presence in Space – as Space, which allows life to take form, and become all that we experience as the physical world, the Earth and the Cosmos. It is for this reason she is called the Divine Mother, the Womb of Space, and the Great Fertile Ocean." (From the Book – Patterns of Creation by Stephen Pope.)*

Mary as Bride: As the Bride she is called Mary Magdalene: In Hebrew *Migdal* means 'tower,' 'fortress:' that is, a deepening awareness of inner creative strength and conscious presence that exists as your core or essence. In Aramaic (spoken Hebrew), 'Magdala' means 'tower' and 'elevation, to grow great, and magnificence.' This means to grow great and to elevate consciousness in the spiritual sense.

Magdalene symbolises an elevated place of consciousness where you can see with clarity of vision, and the power and strength to hold space, in which creativity can take place in each moment. It also represents the central conduit of consciousness within the six directions of space, connecting the I AM presence with spirit (the formless), soul (form), and matter (the body).

Mary Magdalene represents your initiation into higher awareness. This often comes as a result of changes taking place in your life that are not always comfortable. However, such changes are necessary as they open the way to the realisation of a greater consciousness than the mind, and deepening awareness of the universal creative powers of life flowing through you.

She is the path, or way, of honesty spoken about in various biblical stories. She is the stillness behind all movement; supporting all life. When you silence the mind, you begin to notice that all movement continually emerges out of this stillness: the creative powers of the universe expressing themselves continuously through the diversity of all life. Through the conscious breath, you begin to feel that you are intimately connected to the whole of life. (From the teachings in Patterns of Creation).

Signs and symbols are a part of humanity with different cultures having different emblems – we just wanted to share a few of the more common in case the meanings sparked something in you.

PART ONE

WHAT DOES MOTHER
MEAN TO YOU?

IN CONVERSATION
WITH MOTHERS

Setting the Intention – Sarah Lloyd

When we talk of Mothers within this book we are referring to a person who has birthed a child, idea, business – a creatrix of life.

When I received the call from *Wake Up Mother* I knew it needed to be a collaboration.

I saw it very clearly.

Yes, I needed to share the learnings and lessons I was personally moving through, but the vision was a coming together of Mothers, who had each experienced the journey of Mother very differently.

After a few years of procrastinating over whether it was a good idea, I decided to set the intention.

It was in fact, on one of the many walks taken in Winchester with Nicola Humber of the Unbound Press, I got firm guidance to get started and to call in collaborators in the circles around me.

I put sonars out in my circles of women and friends, on social media. And some I knew well, leapt at the chance to share, passionate about their own work.

Other women I didn't know directly soon started to seek me out, too.

At points, I worried it wasn't diverse enough, or representative of other cultures.

'Later....' was the guidance when I sat with it one day.

'This is the beginning,' she shared with me.

And so, followed many conversations until we landed on the solid 13 who participated in a major way.

These women, all in differing stages of their journey, I feel represent just some of the many facets of Mother in a beautiful way.

There were others, who felt drawn to share and some joined us for our community conversations, but they felt they needed to move through something before they could share, or timing-wise it just didn't stack up.

A huge believer of trust and Divine timing, I now see a bigger picture and know there will be plenty of opportunities for those others to share at a later date.

This process of coming together was the start of the medicine of this book, our 'Mothers meet' complete.

So we, as a collective of 'Mothers,' came together regularly to create this collaboration of stories, wisdom and guidance. We began our journey on the 2nd February 2022 (all the twos... if you are into angel numbers!)

This first section of the book hopes to capture just some of the magic that was shared as we sat in circles together.

The answer to the question, 'What does Mother mean to you...?' brought up so many connotations.

The hugeness of that question was not lost on any of us.

Whilst in the dictionary it is boiled down to the act of giving birth to children, and whilst the Rite of Passage of giving birth to another human is huge and has been a point of awakening for so many (me included), it is so much more than that. It is here we share the real and rawness of our responses to that question.

Mother, we ascertained, was not limited to birthing humans. Many of us within this book have children, and share our Motherhood journeys around birth, parenting and death; to showcase the many facets of Mother. There are women included in this book who are not Mothers of physical children, but are Mothers of ideas, businesses and fur babies. There are those who have either chosen to focus their creative Mother Energy on supporting and nurturing others. Or are preparing the path to step into their Mother.

Our conversations around 'What does Mother mean to you?' became a rich tapestry – discussions around real and raw topics.

A showcase of the power of the circle energy, and the weavings that occur when Mothers honour their creatrix energy and meet in a loving, supportive space.

For too long, these conversations have been stopped, moderated, edited and diverted.

In this space, we tumbled over and explored all kinds of subjects. Triggers were activated and then moved through, with no judgment or fear.

There is a reason for the 'Mother's meeting.'

The depiction of the Witches Coven. The Mummy clique.

For years, these places have had a bad rap. But it has always been the women or the Mothers who gathered to create.

These conversations became a reimagining. We were in it together.

A way to view these spaces through a new lens, so they become safe for 'Mothers' to share, in that any triggers and wounds can be healed in these spaces.

Not the hotbed of gossip, backbiting or competitive places so often these spaces became.

Healing the sister wounds that hold us back from meeting others where they are, from joining communities or spaces that trigger us.

Moving to straightening others' crowns and cheering each other on.

It was also a space where we each held each other, during the coming together of this community. There was deep loss of parents moving on for some of our authors, the collective grief around losing the Queen – the patriarchal representation of Mother – and there was shared elation of taking up space for ourselves meeting in person at self-care retreats, festivals and days out.

It's that knowing that when you are having a bad day, someone else in your circle will have the capacity to lovingly 'Mother' you – hold you in your pain – just by being.

And in turn, on the good days, laugh at jokes until you cry with laughter and wet your pants in the process.

We'd love to share with you the intention we set when we began this journey so you can really start to connect with the energies that wanted to come through for you.

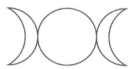

We call in the energy of Imbolc, the energy of the Lunar New Year

I'd love for you to imagine, that we are standing in a circle, in the lush greenness of Mother Earth – in a beautiful sunny meadow, amongst a stone circle deep in the midst of a dark green forest, or on the shores of a beach with the crashing waves a sound track to this intention.

Notice the nature all around us.

We honour the earth, the air, the fire and water that are circulating and supporting us.

As we reach for each other's hands, we feel the fizz of the energy sparking between us.

We may not know each other well yet, but we know each other deep deep down.

Tune into that knowing, that remembering.

As we sway softly in the breeze, leaning into each other's energy, it pulses through us like a collective heartbeat.

We feel all the sisters, on the edges of our circle, those who join us honouring the Mother.

We feel our ancestors are present, helping us to remember, to honour all that has gone before, and start to create waves of healing for generations to come.

Thank you, thank you, thank you.

And so it is.

One thing that each of us who gathered had in common, is we had big awakening moments in our move into the Mother Energy.

Some of us experienced in our rite of passage of stepping into Mother, something that cracked us open... whether it was a difficult birth or pregnancy, postnatal depression, the loss of a parent, bumps in our parenting or business journey, or our re-imagining of what 'Mother' looks like.

As presenced earlier, many of us who have contributed to this book have created businesses or offerings as a result of stepping into our Mother Energy.

We have collectively found that the societal constructs we are living in, just don't allow us to honour the Mother Energy or Motherhood.

You can see this shift occurring, if you follow the news and influencers in the mainstream, to see that the worm is turning.

In the UK @MotherPukka's campaign around flexible working for parents is a great example of this. She is shouting from the rooftops about how Mothers should be celebrated and encouraged back into the workforce, but societal constructs in the workplace just don't support that. And as we wrote this book a bill for a four day working week was passed. In addition @pregnant_then_screwed's #MarchofTheMummies took to the streets to fight for better rights for anyone in the caring sector – midwives, nursing, social care and childcare.

The wonderful Naomi Stadlen, author of *What Mothers Do* and Motherhood guru, who has been talking to Mothers for 30 years, said it so well at the time of writing this, *"Mothering is extremely intelligent. It requires a lot of thought and is hugely underestimated. People trivialise what it is."*

Naomi also shared, *"Until women talk to one another, instead of competing... respect one another and see what other Mothers are doing... they will be stuck in this position of not knowing."*

Motherhood is a huge change of identity; many people are very shaken by it. But if you can survive and hold on, your identity isn't gone, it's just got an additional aspect to it, a new dimension."

Mothers, creators are standing up and being counted.

They are sharing their voices, they are speaking up when old ways are no longer serving them. It is a re-evolution.

TV shows and films are being produced and aired, where the Mother is celebrated and respected. Pointing out the fact that so many of us only behave in the way we have been brought up.

There is so much advice, guidance and wisdom bubbling up. The best bit, most of us are not telling Mothers what to do. They are being guided back to the inner voice – the intuition – the part of us long ago buried and hidden from view.

We have been taught to follow the advice; the step-by-step processes spoon fed to us by the patriarchy.

We have been taught to nod and smile and do what we are told.

Lip service is paid to 'a Mother's intuition;' and as our shares unearthed, that even when we did try to follow our inner knowing or instinct, health and education professionals, societal pressures, even our own (and other) Mothers sought to undermine that inner compass.

Now is the time for Mothers, witches, to reclaim that part long ago squashed. To speak up. To listen to, and more importantly actually follow our intuition.

Time for women in their Mother Energy to no longer sit in the shadows, time to honour the Mother part of our journey.

We are by no means experts (on paper). But you could argue that living and navigating through the Mother Energy; sharing from our scars as opposed to our wounds so others can feel supported, inspired and never alone, helps us to stay curious but wise, as we navigate this path together.

Dulcie, one of our contributors @joyfullmamas; is a birth empowerment coach. A Mother to four beautiful children, her own Mother passed when she was pregnant with her first born. Dulcie shares some of her journey in her own chapter, but speaking into the piece around a Mothers intuition, she helps to guide Mothers who are moving through the various stages of pregnancy. So they feel strong, and no matter how they birth, it is a positive experience for them and their children.

Her Mama sadly never met any of Dulcie's children. And losing her Mama whilst pregnant, Dulcie moved from a place of sadness and deep grief, to alchemising that feeling, and using that fuel to do good. So she is now the person who she wanted so much, back then. For Dulcie stepping into Mother, she wanted to offer that service with such devotion and love.

For Sacred Expression artist, Zoë Foster, the Mother Wound runs deep. Her relationship with her own Mother is superficial at best. Whilst she navigated through postnatal depression with her own children, a likely hangover from her own Mother. Having children meant she could be the Mother she never felt she had, as she never really knew what Mother looked like.

"I've had chronic ill health since I was a baby. And basically, I've done light years of healing in the last decade. And I know so much of that wasn't just the physical. Changing the physical aspects of what I was eating, or supplements, or the things I was doing with my body even – so much of it was an emotional healing crisis related to my relationship with my Mum, my birth – how she basically didn't hold me as a baby. My brother looked after me! All of those things I recognise have such a huge impact upon my physical, mental, emotional and spiritual wellbeing."

Which is why Zoë now expresses herself and teaches others to fully embody and express through her art and through her 'Sacred Expression' work with others.

*"For me, this microcosm of being a Mother, and how society treats us as Mothers, is reflected in the macrocosm at large. And it's so topical right now – I hate that word – but it's so needed right now and it is the right time to address it because everything is being revealed and uncovered, and one **most** definitely will impact upon the other. It's not just that we're speaking to physical Mothers of children, it's that we're speaking to the planet, the universe, as a Mother being, and how we treat that, ultimately."*

Katherine Crawley is another of our authors who teaches other women to embody their feminine energy, after many years of being a yogi, teaching yoga of many different types. She says that around five years ago, she hadn't really understood the power that a woman holds and that first and foremost she is a woman.

"I have been on a long journey of discovering that first and foremost, I'm a woman. The whole journey of womb healing, womb awakening – a deep sensitisation in my body started to take place, which has been phenomenal. And more than anything has shifted my own view to a wider view and kind of presence in this life. It's also shifted my relationship with my husband totally."

Mother to two boys, she is surrounded by the masculine.

"Life has transformed. Now I know what it feels like to be a woman in a woman's body. And what I'm realising is that actually, I'm still at this place, where it is okay to be a Mother. And it feels like in this next piece, for me,

really being a woman is embodying this – this Motherhood Energy. I can't believe, and it's hard for me to say with these two beautiful boys in my life, that I still haven't fully embodied or totally allowed myself to put that first or to operate from that place, first and foremost. Because there's still this judgment that you need to be showing up in 'this way' or 'that way' in the world. I'm being so called now and I can feel the struggle within myself, but I'm being so called to just be present with Motherhood. Because I know that Motherhood energy is not just about Mothering my boys, it's about Mothering my community. It's about Mothering the world. It is the healing energy that is needed for Mother to come on Mother Earth, to come back into alignment.

Aimee Strongman is another yogi. Her children are very small. An ex-school teacher who was on maternity leave with her second child during the Pandemic, she saw an opportunity to build community for Mothers who felt disconnected.

She was the inspiration behind the definition of Mother at the beginning of this book.

"I wrote a definition of Mother, after being inspired by your last Zoom call. So I'm really happy to share that and maybe use that as a kind of catalyst. I used the noun Mother, and took it from there. So... a Goddess on Earth, a female figure of authority, the holder of the hearth, space weaver and one who tends to the inner wisdom and knowing, a soothsayer who illuminates, protects and nurtures others."

She shared this with us. *"I was really inspired by a post I saw on Mother's Day and when I read it back, I really liked the idea that you can be maternal without being a Mother and you can still be, in that seat of Motherhood without having children. It's actually really nice that it doesn't mention anything about children.*

This talks into caregiving, that kind of nurturing, that nourishment. And so it just got me thinking."

This then led Jennifer Flint @wildegg, celebrant and author, to share her experience. In particular, choosing a road less travelled or celebrated – that of the childfree life. Jennifer has published a novel called Wild Egg, inspired by her own seven year journey of answering the question, "Do I want to have children?"

She shares, "*When faced with that question, I thought, 'At the weekend, I'll just do a pros and cons list, no problem.' And I basically fell like Alice down a very deep dark rabbit hole, and never really came out, in a way.*

I think, once I finally decided that Motherhood wasn't my path, I was left with a kind of fertile void in my life. So I went on a bit of a quest to understand what does a meaningful life look like then if I'm not going to have children?

And then the thing that came up immediately, as I embarked to find the answer to that, was this feeling that I had Motherhood Energy.

I've never heard anyone use the term before that. I didn't even really know what I was talking about, to be quite honest. But I just had this very powerful sense of having Motherhood Energy, that somehow needed to be expressed.

And since then, I guess I've probably been on a journey to understand what does that mean and how do I manifest that in some way in my life?

And I think when I thought about the word Mother, I saw something quite visual – metaphoric – that idea of a womb or an egg. So I thought about Mother as a container – that Mother is a safe space. Mother is a holder of something. Then also, I had an idea of this wild energy as well. Something quite untamed, something very fierce and wild and primal, like pure creative force.

There's something paradoxical – of this loving space and this wild energy – that also cracks that open at the same time.

So I think, for me, being Mother there's something about nurturing, birthing and creativity, as a force that rips through things and rips through this idea of what we're 'meant,' what we 'should do,' – that we should tune back into nature. Something grounded, something like howling at the moon!"

Ceryn Rowntree @thedivinefeminist, author, medium, soul-led coach and space holder, picked up on Jennifer's thread regarding our rite of passage into Mother and honouring our cycles.

"I think if we go back in time, to a point when we actually honoured the cycles of our lives, we honoured the phases of our lives. That step into Motherhood was a rite of passage.

Being a Mother was what it was to be effectively a mature woman, to be a conscious woman, to be a space holder, to be a nurturer, all those things. It did not mean having to give birth to a child.

Yes, you could birth a child and many people would of course, but as I'm in a different position, in that I very much want to have children, but it hasn't happened for me, yet. And so I find myself in a really interesting place actually, where a lot of people will look at me and go, 'Oh, well, she doesn't want children.'

But they may not consider that, no, no, that's because she hasn't had them yet. No, that's not the case. It's just a different situation.

And again, it's breaking out of those bonds of society. But now I think we have reached this point where what we see is how to be in that phase of Motherhood.

In that... society impresses on women that... you must have had a child. And almost then it goes to the 'nth degree, because then we get these people who go, 'You must have birthed a child;' 'You must have naturally given birth to a child,' 'You must breastfeed'...and then we just keep breaking it down more and more and more to become a smaller and smaller box.

But actually, if we go right back, the physical act of birthing a child – if indeed you did that – after that, came the rite of passage and Motherhood.

So the physical act of birthing a child was not in itself the rite of passage of Motherhood. And I think we have a great big problem in society, at this point in time, because we completely conflate the two.

For some people absolutely birthing a child will be an awakening, that in itself will be its own rite of passage.

But it doesn't have to be the rite of passage and the marker of maturity for a woman. I read a piece from a writer called Laura McCowan a few years ago who talks about sobriety.

Some people say that having a baby and becoming a Mother was the thing that changed their life. Laura explains that for her it wasn't. Whilst she was a Mother for many years, what changed her life was actually getting sober. It was interesting to watch the comments, because a lot of people have also shared that they wholeheartedly agree. A lot of other people had said, 'No, not for me. It was having my child.'

And then other people have shared with me – I had a child, I got sober, but the awakening, the change in me came with something else.

We've just got this conflated idea of birth, of birthing, as being the only rite of passage into female maturity and into womanhood.

And for me, that is quite sad for those women who don't want to have children, who can't have children. But it's also quite dangerous for children because you're putting a lot of onus on a child to be the one who awakens their Mother.

When actually the journey is, we all need a 'Wake up Mother' moment ourselves. We wake up, and that's how we become Mothers. And then that's how – if we indeed birth children – that's how we become the best Mothers we can be.

This idea that children aren't always the point in which we move into Mother was talked into in some depth. Some of the authors in this book felt the call when giving birth and for others, whilst children and businesses were playing a part in the rite of passage to Mother, it was something else entirely.

For Kathy Bell, a breathwork facilitator, space holder, and Mother of one; she described her 'awakening' or rite of passage to becoming Mother when she gave birth to her daughter.

"When I gave birth to my daughter, I had the most electric, amazing bolt of lightning awakening experience. I was lit from the inside when she was crowning. I'll never forget that experience. It changed me."

And then I don't know if any of you have ever read the book, 'Anna, Grandmother of Jesus.' I read this book all the time. I've been reading it probably on and off the last five years. In one of the very first chapters, Anna, Grandmother of Jesus, or the Mother of Mary, talked about how she was the oversoul, and how she inhabits the physical body of this girl called Anna.

Just the way she describes it, I was just like, "Well, that's what happened to me." I still don't fully understand it. But I believe at that moment when I was in the pool, and in the midst of all the people around me, some aspects of my oversoul entered my being. I became more of an embodied version of myself.

And then there is the physical journey of Motherhood. Which is quite complex. It's not that I don't have a great relationship with my Mother, but we are very separate. I've had to learn to Mother myself. She's a great Grandmother, and she's always been there for me financially. But in terms of that deep bond, we don't have that.

My personal experience with becoming a Mother was really challenged by the passing of my father-in-law, two months after my daughter was born. So there's just this whole thing. I wasn't a single parent, but I was a single parent, because the rest of my family were dealing with this huge grief, including my husband.

So becoming a Mother for me, well there's a lot of grief around that, because it didn't happen as I wanted it to. In my mind, it was hard to compute... why was everyone so upset? I just had a baby. That was a juggle in so many ways.

All of this has led me to connect with the energy of Mother Mary. Mother Mary, is the Mother of Mothers. So I work with her energy. I'm getting so emotional, sorry. Her energy in essence, is here with us and will flow through this. She is after all the ultimate space holder, so I feel her holding our space as we travel to a deeper level."

Kathy shares more on her experience in her chapter.

As we moved through our circle of 13 – a potent number for women – Clara Apollo, broadcaster and Qigong master teacher and single Mother to a grown up son, shared her experience.

"A rich cauldron we have here, and how connected we all already are. I am recognising myself in your stories. And that's what this is about, isn't it?

Sharing our stories and noticing how much we have in common, even though we have different aspects of the story, is that Mother.

How friggin common, is that sadly in the generations before and when I was bringing up my boy, I was absolutely determined to not be the Mother that I was Mothered by.

I might have gone too much the other way. He's 33 now, and we have quite a mixed relationship. As I've been growing as a woman, he's struggled. I used to respond differently to some of the triggers, and now because I am where I am, I mostly don't rise to them anymore. And he doesn't know what to do.

I have gone through a lot of pain to be able to get to that point and we've had different ups and downs through our journey... So again, that's part of the story, I guess, of being a Mother through the ages.

As a group we paused and spoke on, how as Mother, we are the ones who need to be flexible; ebb and flow with the tide. In some cases, that was the differing stages of our children's development; for others it was working with seasonal changes and our own seasons and cycles.

"You know I always wanted a baby," said Kathy. *"But now I have a 10 year old, there is almost this part of us that forgets that long term we are going to end up with a 10 year old and no longer have a baby."*

"Or a 33 year old man," shared Clara. "We have to change our Mothering approach, because they grow older. And of course, we don't change at all. But we've got what's going on with us, moving through our own stuff. So that's been fascinating, and it's still going on. You never stop being a Mum, you never stop, but the apron strings are longer. And the conversations are more adult. It's also easier to call him out on his bullshit now."

"I think that trusting the Mothering inside, trusting what we give to ourselves as a fundamental before anything else, is what my Qigong practice has shown me over the years. So I'm an elemental Qigong teacher and trainer and have been for 20-odd years. I've always been interested in the energies that we can't see.

We can feel the language of truth behind everything. And shamanic practice training as well. I originally trained as a nurse, but that's another story.

I wanted to share a moment in time that seems poignant to our conversation as it flows. I was living in a little beach hut on a cliff in Cornwall, without any tech. So I was really isolated and moving through menopause. I loved being in amongst the elemental energy of the water and being held by the cliff.

I knew that I needed to be in that space to take me deep into what I was searching for, which was how do I Mother myself?

So I posed the question to the Great Grandmother underneath our feet. I'm deeply grateful to connect with her all the time. Whenever I am in any doubt, there she is, presencing that rooting, that energy connection, that physical connection, that power, that sound, the colours, the richness of the Earth and how she's fine, the Earth is fine.

She's just having to do all this because the humans are struggling. And that wisdom of the Great Mother, if I can even get an inkling of that within me, *then that nourishes me. That brings me back into myself, and I begin to say to myself, okay, I am balanced, I am connected. I am nature, she is nature, we are all nature. Let's just regain that reality, that truth that is within us, an entity. Now what stories come from there and how we can support onwards and forwards? I could wax on about that. And I actually don't think I've ever spoken quite like this before."*

As we discussed stories similar to Clara's; one thing that came up as we journeyed through the conversation: Mothers need other Mothers in community.

We also all found peace within when taking time out for ourselves to connect with the Earth.

"My own experience," said Sarah Lloyd. *"Which also came up when I had the idea to create this beautiful circle and the book you hold in your hands, I'd love to share with you...*

I was sitting on the beach. It was day two of our holiday and it was post the first lockdown and before the second. And I was just done. It was something like 6 am and I needed space so I headed to the beach for a walk and a sit.

I was watching the world wake up, sitting on the rocks and watching the tide come in, and that's when I realised. Us humans, we're like those little teenagers that slam the door after a row with our parents. We stamp our feet and have our tantrums, and the Mother is still always there.

It doesn't matter what we do or say to her. She's still there. She still holds our space. Without question. The leaves still fall, the flowers still bloom.

And that for me was a huge realisation. It mirrored back to me what we experience as Mothers of businesses and of children. That it is our job to stay rooted and grounded; while the tantrums rage on. It is our job to be the stillness; the port in the storm and the place to go for love.

When I personally went through pregnancy, postnatal depression (PND); there was a splintering. I feel depression is the wrong word maybe; it felt like a part of me had fallen away, ceased to exist and left in that space was a new raw version of me. I think Ceryn referenced it earlier in our discussion; but I never felt I had the mental tools or information to confidently step into this new version of me. So I tried to continue to be the old me; with a baby. And of course you can't continue to operate that way. Something invariably has to give.

My parents tried to help me the best they could – I actually couldn't hear a lot of what they were trying to share with me. It wasn't until I woke up – I realise that Mum probably saw, in what I was moving through, some of the challenges she had with me. Being a much younger Mum, I suspect she found it hard and frustrating to parent me. I know now she had PND with me, and I suspect that my Grandmother may have also had it too. Possibly that is part of it. I see myself mirroring that lineage at times.

What is lovely, though, is I can now see it. And with Mum's guidance, I am approaching things in a different way. My Mum came from an era, the youngest of seven, she spent the whole of her life being told that she was less than – she was the youngest of the family.

And I feel my Mum and I have started to do the work to reframe our patterns for the future generations to come," said Sarah. *"I think that's when the healing with my Mother came."*

"I would love this to be a book that would be there for all of the different stages of your Motherhood journey," shared Kathy. *"One that you could pass to your sister and you'd share it with your friends and it would come*

back to you, and they would then get their own copies, like that kind of timelessness to it because being a Mother never really stops."

The following insights are key points that were raised in circle conversations which feel important to include and share...

I think part of my story might help, not only the women that are here, but other women, to share our stories, that have helped us and then to inspire one another. It's like we're calling the stories from one another, through these conversations, I'm learning, and in turn I think I might help others," said Sarah. "The feeling that collectively we can provide medicine here through our stories, is a feeling so strong in my heart right now."

"And not forgetting that wisdom was shared through the ages. In a village community, women did sit in a circle, sharing their wisdom and knowledge passed down. There was a red tent," said Katherine. *"Menstruation was honoured and it was a powerful time. A woman's intuition was seen as a Goddess-like power.*

Intuition is something that is making a re-appearance quite fiercely. We want to turn the dial up on that. It's a collective remembering isn't it?"

Motherhood has no manual. And there is a tendency to bypass this rite of passage. It is important that we claim it with reverence. So in the retreats that I do, the essence is reverence for my presence, and I love the honouring in that. I feel that collectively, we can bring that to the table so beautifully," said Dulcie. "So people remember it, and the deepness of the experience is really felt and honoured and passed on.

Yeah, I love that you touched on the intergenerational aspect of Mother, which is so potent, so powerful. And it ties together all of those threads of, as you say, each of the stages where we feel lost," said Aimee Strongman.

"We feel lost when we start puberty as a woman, because it's like this massive change in our society. And when I was a kid, it really wasn't talked about, or if it was, it was horrific," shared Clara.

"It was the curse – it was all those things. And now, I feel like we're actually starting to remember, reclaiming that maternal and that Divine Feminine energy, all of it together."

"I think that's the thing about the patriarchal society we live in.

Even from when you're pregnant, everything is monitored, and it's processed, and it's boxed. And you go in and give birth, and you're either in trouble because you're breastfeeding, or you're in trouble because you're bottle feeding, then it's like you're stuck on a conveyor belt," said Emma While.

"So all of our wisdom that we hold, not just our own, but our ancestral wisdom, that we hold in our bodies – all of that is gaslit. Because we have science, we have checkboxes, we have procedures, all of that. Our wisdom, our art, that we hold within us, it's so ancient and it's there, and we can just tap into it. It's not in our heads, it's in our bodies. And that's a really beautiful, expansive, incredible thing to share, isn't it, for people to witness and realise and feel?" said Zoë.

Yeah. And it's about the feeling. I think that's the thing. It's like we forgot. Like you were saying, they'll see the remembering of listening to our intuition and our knowing, and that does get gaslit out of us," said Emma While.

"It's not just as a Mother, in the physical sense, either though, is it? For example, I would often get gaslit in a business situation – especially when I was following my intuition or gut. It comes back to process... 'Why have you done it this way?' 'Why don't you tick that box?' 'Why are you working in this fluid way?' And they don't understand that working in a fluid way, or birthing or whatever it is that we're creating, needs space to manifest," shared Sarah.

We need both sets of energy and I feel like we want to honour that Motherhood Energy, but also understand that there are some ways where we can help ourselves more.

For example, my husband would come in to take over from me, when he'd get in from work. He was just so nurturing and loving, and I would find myself getting so angry at him, myself, literally saying, "Why are you a better parent than me?" It sounds ridiculous when I say it! "Why are you parenting our child better than me? Why are you nurturing her better than me?"

I always felt like the worst parent, like I was doing it wrong, almost resentful of them both. But what I didn't appreciate is I hadn't given myself permission to stop and rest and allow space. And actually nine hours of parenting is a lot – and of course he was going to come in all fresh and loving after a day in the office. And that's totally normal!

I think it's so ingrained in us that we need to constantly be on top of our game 24/7. And it's absolutely not possible," said Sarah.

"And then it's impossible, **impossible**. The wheels fall off. And they did fall off for me," said Debra Munro, founder of the Lace Knittery.

"My children are in their 20s. And I went through all the same sort of things – 'I'm not good enough.' And 'I'm not doing everything.' And 'I'm not doing this.'

I felt like I was going to have a nervous breakdown. And my husband was working away half the week, every week. So on my own with nobody, basically because we had to move around a lot for work.

Their experience of that situation was very different. They'll tell me that they loved it when we had picnic teas on the carpet, or something else I'd done on the fly to just cope. I was trying to cope, they saw and experienced something different. They saw a brilliant Mother. They loved it.

And I'm like, "You have no idea, absolutely no idea!" at that point.

So your kids wouldn't have seen any of that. And that's why we're so hard on ourselves. We're terrible. And even though I'm getting better, I'm still terrible. I'm so bad at it. But we've got to forgive ourselves. I think it's one of the big things."

Rachel Haywood, shared, "Yeah, that's the thing about not having a handbook, because I was a single Mum and my son's Dad left when he was two and a half.

But there was always that thing, whenever he went to his Dad, it always seemed like he did all the fun stuff with him.

And he came back to me with rules. 'It's boring with Mum, we don't go to Disney World.' How do you manage that?"

"My thoughts were all about... 'If I can just get us through the day,'" said Debbie Munro. "And we have food, and we're warm and we've got clothes. Bottom line, if that was taken care of, then I knew I was doing all right.

Katherine responded, "Ironically, that perpetuates a version of the Mother Wound because if your needs are not getting met, you're going to act out because you're going to try and get those needs met in some way. And that is then reflected upon your kids. And it goes on and on and on. And so it's up to us if we're going to heal that.

It's up to us to nourish and protect ourselves and have those boundaries and model them.. Not perfectly, definitely not perfectly. But yes, model them with integrity."

"And it really struck me, earlier in our conversation," said Katherine. "Someone said the word 'perfect.' Motherhood isn't perfect. The journey into Motherhood isn't easy."

There is an expectation that you have to be this perfect Mother, you have to be this perfect partner, you have to be this perfect, size 10, six foot blonde, whatever it is. We are given all of these by society, this perfect little box that we have to fit in. And Motherhood can't be put in a box, in any shape, or form; it evolves and grows and develops."

"Motherhood is celebrated in other cultures, but not in Western society.

"We are reclaiming something about the Celtic tradition in the UK, that is being called through all of us women right now," said Ceryn. "It's like reclaiming what we have, when we look at other indigenous communities.

The land that remembers our souls.

Remember, we've been called together. This is part of it, reclaiming women's wisdom and the wisdom of their cultures that have gone before us, before they were wiped out by the bloody Romans."

PART TWO

MOTHERS' STORIES

ANSWERING THE CALL

By Sarah Lloyd
Mother of two girls and Mother of IndigoSoulPR.

I was in the shower when I heard the words, 'Wake Up Mother.'

I was actually having a quiet cry while the water thundered around my ears, because I was ridiculously tired. We were in the midst of lockdown 1.0 and I'd reached the end of my tether. The girls were always early birds, and super light sleepers. I'd been sneaking down at 4am to try and keep on top of my fledgling business and client work; and be present for them in the day time.

In that snatched moment, a stream of downloads then followed. It was at that moment, I realised I needed to stop playing the victim to this role I had desperately asked for.

To do better. Be better.

Find that emotional maturity I needed, to be the Mother I wanted to be and that my children needed.

The pity party for one, all but dried up at that moment.
It was like someone had slapped me round the face and woke me up.

Of course, that version of myself still resurfaces even now, but it was the wake-up call I needed to help me to be more conscious as a Mother of children, and a Mother of my business.

Navigating two years of home schooling, mediating, endless cooking, and cleaning, nurturing frayed nerves, managing big feelings and developing minds, being the calm, safe, space in the madness; was a fast track in emotional maturity, if ever there was one.

The downloads that I received that day in the shower advised me that this would need to be a book, a movement, a celebration of all that is Mother.

Not just the physical act of giving birth to children – that definition is one dimensional and does not capture all there is, to be a woman in her Mother's energy.

The whispers in the shower were telling me to wake up to the possibility of embracing another way of being.

To honour the Mother's energy.

To flow with it, not fight it.

Life as we know it is out of balance. Women have got it wrong.

We are fighting for equality that will never exist.

We are not men's equals. We are their partners.
  Yin to the Yang. Sun to the Moon.

When we find that unity, that beautiful harmony of unconditional love for one another, THAT is the balance that we are actually searching for.

We have spent centuries fighting for equality.

Wanting the same as men. Wanting to be like men.

Our bodies are so fucking confused.

From the beginning of our journey into Mother, we try to control our bodies.

We exercise like men, and take pills to control our emotions, our menstrual cycle, pregnancy and everything in between. Then at the other end take more tablets to control our rite of passage from Mother to Crone.

We try to stay young; the beauty industry and social media has so much to answer for; as does Hollywood and the music industry. We are brought up with unrealistic role models and this perpetual search for the fountain of youth.

It is instilled in us from a young age – Barbie and Disney have A LOT to answer for. From a young age, it is drilled into us that our job is to be young and attractive for the opposite sex. Keeping us in our Maiden for as long as possible.

Then when we hit our Mother, the gear changes. We then have to be the perfect mum for our kids... PTA, bake sales, the costumes for the school play... all this as well as keeping our relationships going, and a house and our careers afloat. With booze being the medicine that keeps that engine going.

If that isn't enough – when we hit our wisdom we are essentially cast aside, destined to play the cat lady, crazy aunt or the withered old witch.

The recognition of success in our society, being marked in making money and having all the things – including the perfect house, children and picket fence.

These are patriarchal constructs.

Women are strong.

Women are capable.

They are feisty, curious, outspoken, and can be whoever the fuck they want to be.

If they choose to follow the path of bearing children, or decide that their destiny lies elsewhere, likely birthing an idea, a business, nurturing other women and children... then that should be embraced. Creation is at the root of all.

We, the womb carriers, are the creators of life, new ideas, new ways.

The womb is where our wisdom lies.
 Our wisdom has been suppressed, stifled, boxed in. Even now the dominance over women's bodies rages; with patriarchal ideas managing our cycles, and even having an opinion over our wombs... stifling talk around emotions and hormones.

This runs so deep in our conditioning. And we thought we lived in a progressive world. But then I sit and think, I am so lucky to be here now, so I can be a catalyst for change, for future generations.

That said, have you ever had a male boss, and called in sick with 'women's problems'... the phone call would get shut down in seconds. None of us, the women included, able to talk about something so natural, whispering in toilets together.

I remember when I became a Mother to my girls.

I was prepared on a practical level. I had all the stuff, the nursery was organised, the babygros were washed and ironed (I know, WTAF!) the childcare picked out. I read all the books, talked to my friends about children and went to NCT.

I was not prepared at all for the shift in me.

One thing I found – no-one ever really tells you the truth – not until much later – when your physical scars are healing, and you can handle it; or you simply have the bandwidth to absorb it.

They never share that when you are waddling about with a baby pushing your veins out of your legs, you feel horny and lush and sexy some days and like a whale on legs, other days.

They never share with you that every time your baby cries, your womb contracts and your boobs leak or just swell into hard rocks of pain. That breastfeeding is not easy for everyone – in fact it is hell on Earth. Some of us just aren't able to do it and that really is OK! And no amount of manhandling in the hospital is going to change that. That if you choose to breastfeed, the hell of finding the 'right' and comfortable position for both of you.

I remember one snot-filled 3 am feed, where we were both crying, because I was too tired and sore to figure out the latch. My husband essentially had to position me and the baby (because he had listened to the midwife) which in itself was a humiliating moment for me – I felt a huge failure.

No-one ever mentioned that you go from your boobs not wanting to play, to leaking all over the floor, the minute you jump out of the shower – the smell of gone off milk following you around all day.

And don't get me started on the other end. I had a C-section. And you still suffer with incontinence; bleed like a mofo and have piles that resemble blueberries. I only carried one at a time, I cannot imagine and must tip my hat to any Wonder Woman carrying more than one child or who ripped a new hole!

No, they just look at you knowingly and tell you to enjoy this time – you'll never get that time back. And make sure you sleep when the baby sleeps.

I also got told to listen to your intuition – Mother knows best. But whose Mother? My intuition often went against what the books and midwives and sometimes my husband and my own Mother were telling me.

The battle of who knew best was very real for me. I didn't have a friggin clue!

It's not just about giving physical birth. Whilst that in itself was a wondrous but painful time, what I didn't realise was that bringing a being into the world who I literally loved more than myself, meant something had to give.

A part of me had to die. The old Sarah had to make way for the new Sarah.

The penny really only dropped for me when I started working with energy.

What I mean by that, is essentially your child (business /fur baby) is an extension of you and your energy. If you are in a bad mood and tired, guaranteed they are also in a bad mood and tired. It was like looking in a mirror.

It also meant that new Sarah had to woman up and parent old Sarah, whilst parenting two small humans. *All I can say is thank God for Dr Becky Kennedy, author of 'Good Inside,' who taught me something so many of us struggle with. I am good inside; and there are always two things that are true.*

I used to joke about not wanting a small version of myself to taunt me... I have two.

Two miniature feisty, stubborn and wonderful versions of myself constantly showing me where I fuck up as a human – in the nicest way possible.

They are the gifts that keep on giving. Just as you 'master' how to parent a toddler, they become little girls with thoughts and feelings and opinions of their own.

They have also shown me what it is to be a Mother.

It is they who are teaching me how to not only Mother them, but myself too.

As they grow older they need me in different ways.

We are still moving through that as a unit, they are becoming people with thoughts and feelings, which I still struggle with. I find myself regularly in a battle of wills with my girls over different things.

That in itself has taught me to step back and hold their space, while they and I figure it out.

Another thing I have realised is being Mother is often a thankless task.

This I feel does need to change... and I am not saying we need paying or constant empty thank yous... what I mean is a collective acknowledgment or love for the Mother... another reason why I felt called to bring together this collaboration.

Mothers ARE the invisible force that keeps it all together.
 The Cosmic Womb that the unit sits within, as you hold them lovingly.

Mother Earth holds us much in the same way. She ebbs and flows with her seasons and cycles; and occasionally, when it gets too much, she fights back. The floods, the earthquakes, the drying up of resources – strikes me that she is pissed off at us, her children, the parasites that live on her, raping and pillaging and covering her with concrete. This is her sobbing on the toilet as her children wreck her home, she lovingly just cleaned.

I, for one, realised when I became a Mother myself, how much my Mum actually did for me growing up; how much space she held and how often she would be there quietly waiting, whenever I needed her.

I cringe when I think back to how awful I was to her, especially during my teen years, never really understanding that she had feelings too.

Waking up meant I also understood a little better, that my girls are not 'mine.'

They are not possessions (another patriarchal construct).
That I am just simply borrowing them until they become fully interdependent and carve their own way in the big wide world.

Interestingly, I just had to explain this lesson to my own girls when we introduced two guinea pigs into our home.

Seeing that play out was eye-opening, explaining to the girls that they were living animals that needed space, and time to adjust and they were not things they could just discard when bored, and ignore the rest of the time.

It was like talking to my own inner child, about her version of Motherhood – playing house, playing Mum – I guess we are all playing at this...

Of course, all that my girls saw was that they were 'their' pets and they would play with them when they damn well wanted to, regardless of how the guinea pig was reacting.

One guinea pig made its feelings pretty clear to my eldest and they now understand each other (do not try and carry a Guinea pig upside down it will bite you!).

Suffice to say, after working through that with the children, and seeing the lesson I needed to see, because it's always there for us to witness, both parties are relatively happy. With them both still enjoying Mothering the guineas, cleaning out their cage and feeding them their veggies each day.

I've experienced similar lessons through birthing my business.

So how does birthing a business equate to being a Mother then?

Well the definition of Mother is 'to give birth to' or 'to give rise to.' When we create our businesses, ideas or services; they are essentially like children – they are an entity in their own right.

They are created to serve a purpose. They are no longer 'ours;' they require nurturing, guidance and support in their development. They evolve and grow to support the needs and requirements of customers. In marketing campaigns there is something called a 'nurture' sequence which lends itself to keeping our clients happy and sated.

My clients are typically women who have gifts to share with the world. I have supported men too, but I seem to attract mainly women at this stage. And the needs and requirements of those customers vary.

One size never fits all.

My business is another of those service-based dark arts. People know it's kind of important, but don't really know what it is. They just know it helps their business 'get out there.'

I support businesses with their publicity, and to my mind, the simplified definition of that is when someone else says your stuff is good.

It's super powerful when that 'someone else' is a trusted third party – such as the media or an influencer – but even that is dicey ground currently. With the media being accused of not being discerning in its sharing of stories.... That, Dear Reader, is another story.

After a few years of doing what I had always done (unconsciously following a corporate blueprint), it soon dawned on me the whole point of setting up my business was to create something that served both my clients and myself.

Once I had figured out who it was I wanted to support, the types of businesses I wanted to serve, and who also understood my feminine, intuitive approach – I started to attract businesses who worked in a similar way.

What I also realised is many of my clients understand the power of sharing their essence, their story; but it is uncomfortable for them. It is actually uncomfortable for many of us. When we share our truth laid bare in a newspaper, it can bring up all the feels, especially if you are a changemaker wanting to make waves!

Realising that my clients come to me for nurturing and support, whilst sharing their deepest vulnerabilities and their stories in the media, was a huge wake up.

For some, I hold their space for several months, just to get them started and moving in the right direction. Others, we journey together for a while – growing, uplevelling together.

I have also had to get over a 'Mother Wound' around the work I do with clients. And I know this is deep seated in me. It's come up in past life and Akashic journeys I have taken.

When your client appears in the press; but doesn't acknowledge the part we have played. It used to cut really deep. And it lends itself back to the point I made earlier, about the Mother being the silent partner, the strong support, the nurturer and ultimately the one who has to let go, knowing they played an important role and that cycle is complete.

It is like watching your children grow up. Or even learning to ride a bike. There comes a point when they no longer need the stabilisers. And they can ride all on their own.

I have realised, these past few years, when I first heard those words in the shower, it was like a call to arms.

In my business, I enable others to take the next big step in business, through sharing stories to the right people. I Mother them to the next level – that is transformational and important!

In the same way, being a Mother to the next generation is again not something to be sniffed at.

We are all doing the best we can, with the resources we have available.

One thing that did come up this summer is, kids really don't want all the stuff. They want and need your love. That's literally it. Just being there, loving them through it all.

I also recognised something deep inside, something that had been hidden from sight for so long.

That 'Mother' is within us all.

That silent part of ourselves, the nurturer, the support, the quiet unconditional love.

The honouring of that service the Mother Energy brings to society. Well, she no longer should be silent.

And this is my celebration of all that is Mother.

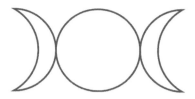

RECLAIMING THE MOTHER:
Breaking free of the cages and definitions of Motherhood to own what is ours

By Ceryn Rowntree

For a long time, I struggled to write this chapter. I've written whole books, yet to write these few thousand words felt impossible.

Why? Because I'm not a Mother – or at least not to a child, meaning that I don't fit the dictionary definition of that word, and just maybe leading many people to think I have nothing to share in this book. Hell, causing some part of me to believe I have nothing to share in this book.

Yet perhaps that's exactly what qualifies me to write a chapter here, to question not only the validity of that idea, but also the validity of so many other judgements we make about ourselves and one another as Mothers and as those who identify as women.

Because for as many times as I've been told over the years that having not yet birthed a child makes me unworthy of claiming the title of Mother, I've also been told that the same factor means I don't know anything about life, about being a woman.

If the judgement stopped there, then maybe I would never have put pen to paper to write this chapter. Maybe I would have settled down into the wound of unworthiness those statements never fail to re-open within me, mourned the children that haven't yet come into my life, and left these pages for those who could truly own that title of Mother in the way that society defines.

But here's the thing: over recent years I've come to realise that societal definition is exclusive of not only those who haven't had children of their own, but so many others besides.

I've had clients who were told they weren't Mothers because their children had come to them through adoption or marriage. One had even overheard a 'friend' say that she shouldn't be called a Mother because she had conceived through IVF.

I know friends who have been told they weren't real Mothers because the arrival of their child had been through surgery rather than natural labour.

Family members whose decision not to breastfeed has led to side-eyes and questions about why they were choosing not to nourish their children properly.

And colleagues whose decision to go back to full-time work led others to ask how it was, not to be a Mother all the time, as though out of sight somehow meant out of mind, enough to forget their children entirely.

Aren't you tired of this constant comparison and belittling of one another? Of the ridiculous, narrow-minded idea of what it means to be a 'real' Mother? Because I sure as hell am.

I'm exhausted from holding others through the tears and anger that follow those conversations, reminding them that no matter what anyone else may say or believe, they are enough.

That so often, the very question of 'Am I a good Mother?' is, in itself an affirmative answer. Because isn't a 'good' Mother one who will do everything in their power to give the entire world and all of its beauty to the little people they are so incredibly fortunate to parent?

I am heartbroken from years of rocking myself to sleep after my own similar conversations, gaslit into wondering whether I truly know what terms like 'love,' 'tired' and 'commitment' mean, since I haven't yet birthed a child. And finding myself, even now, fighting an urge to justify how I know and experience each of those things for myself, and in my own life after so many years of being laughed at by people who told me they knew better.

And, more than any of that, I am sick and frustrated with a single, specific, and often unattainable definition of Motherhood being the job description against which we are judged for not only how we birth and raise our children, but also for how we live our lives – for simply being women out in the world.

Within their books *Womb Magic* and *The Magdalene Mysteries*, Seren and Azra Bertrand write of 'Ma' as an original name for the primordial Goddess – named for the M shape that is visible when someone with a yoni opens their legs and showcases the source of their power. The authors go on to describe the priestesses of that Goddess as carrying not only her powerful and beautiful energy out into the world, but also her name through titles like 'Ma-maids' (later becoming the Mermaids who would seduce men into the watery depths of emotions) and 'Ma-ry' (yes, there is a reason Jesus was surrounded by so many Marys!); through words that would one day lead us to the word Mother.

The truth is this: Motherhood is not something we earn through our relationships to one or more people, but instead one of the most potent facets of feminine energy. But the more we restrict it, with demands upon and definitions of, how it *should* look and what *must* happen in order for us to claim it, the less we truly own that energy, and the less any of us benefit from its power within the world and ourselves.

In the circles that I move in, both spiritual and feminist, we hear about a need to heal the sisterhood wounds that cause us to bitch and compete against one another, so that we can instead stand tall, proud and supportive together. We hear about the need to break free from that good girl conditioning once and for all so that we can be liberated to live like the powerful queens that we are. And we hear about the importance of our claiming every single aspect of the power that is, can be and has always been ours, as women in this world. And using that power to reshape societies that are safer, fairer and more balanced.

For me, every part of that begins with claiming that Mother Energy, no matter who we are and what our circumstances may be.

It begins with reclaiming and honouring the Mother within ourselves; a figure that can create the new wherever it needs to sprout. And who, no matter how that new looks and feels, can nurture it into a beautiful and healthy life through which its highest possibilities can be met. The Mother within reminds us that we are sovereign over our own selves. And sovereign over the choices we make in, not only our bodies but also our hearts, our heads and our lives.

It continues with recognising and honouring the Mother within one another; finding those trusted sisters and not only supporting them and the choices they make from a place of their own sovereignty, but also allowing them to support us. Leaning into the power of community and trusting those who have our backs, are safe enough and supportive enough to hold our hearts and our souls, as they are needed too.

It encompasses listening to, feeling and honouring the collective Mother Energy that rises like rageful fire when we hear about the deaths of children, or the injustices that have been committed against those with less power to affect change. An energy that for too long has been hushed and feared when its ferocity is so often the fuel that guides us to protect and to support what is right and true.

It involves acknowledging and honouring the Mothers that have been; from those who first created and tended upon this planet of ours at a time when that energy could unfold freely, beautifully, and in the fullness of itself; all the way to those in the generations before us, so many of whom have been restricted and tainted by the bonds of patriarchy, by the judgements of others, by the mistaken belief of all that they should be, in order to claim the title of Mother for themselves.

It demands that we encourage and honour the Mothers to come; restraining ourselves from judgement or criticism as they inevitably stumble on the path to find their way. And celebrate them as they not only take the steps that lead them onto the path of Motherhood, but also carve out their own version of that path, even though that may seem wild and unrealistic to our limited minds.

And, perhaps most importantly of all, it asks us to put down our roots and reconnect ourselves to the ultimate Mother, the planet that supports and nurtures us all throughout every moment of these human lives of ours. All while reminding us so clearly that, although She is supporter, protector, nurturer and enchantress in the most potent of ways, She could not and would not fit into that perfect image of Motherhood that we humans seem so determined to inflict upon ourselves and one another.

Yup, I said it, that the unattainable vision of Mother is a cage inflicted upon all of us – by a system that wants us to feel inferior, to separate us from ourselves and one another, and to have us working so hard to reach their idea of perfect, that we are too damned tired to remember the true power of the Mother, and to utilise the potency of that energy in a way that was always meant to be ours.

In her book, *Life's Daughter/Death's Bride*, Kathie Carlson writes about the ways that our patriarchal cultures have severed themselves from all things feminine – something I also talk about in my book *The Divine Feminist* – not least because patriarchy is terrified of the creative power that exists within that feminine energy. It is terrified of the seductive nature of the feminine which inspires the very world to dance to a particular rhythm; and of the deep and nourishing emotional connections that the feminine encourages between people.

And so, Carlson tells us, like Hades in the Greek myth of Persephone and Demeter, patriarchy snatches the fertile Maiden from the nourishing and connected relationship to her Mother – the true feminine. It locks her away in an underworld cage within which she too must suffer that sense of disconnection from her creative power, nature, and the wholeness of life.

Carlson suggests that it is the patriarchal, Hades-like voice within each of us that leads us to judge one another as not enough; to look down upon ourselves and our own actions as being somehow less than they 'should' be; and to doubt our power and abilities enough that we will even turn away from anything that could or would feel truly creative, connected, or fierce, unless those things are firmly deemed acceptable in the cookie cutter models of life and womanhood that society has given us.

It is a voice that each one of us is undoubtedly familiar with. And a voice that is running the show every time we place the idea of Motherhood into a restrictive cage.

But what would it be like, if we were to truly reclaim that label of Mother for all that it once meant. For the power that exists not only when we conceive, birth, or raise a child, but for the very spark of energy that exists within each of us to enable the creativity that conceives the new, the endurance to birth it into the world, the fearlessness which protects what is important to us, and the deeply empathic nurturing which allows that to grow and thrive?

What would it be like if we were to take that spark, that essence of our own innate Motherhood. And, instead of running ourselves into the ground trying to shape it into a particular form, simply allow it to illuminate the path of Motherhood that was always intended to be ours; the unique path that no-one else out there could ever dream of bringing to the world?

Maybe doing that would help us to recognise the beauty and the love that is available from foster Mothers and Aunties – those who may not have birthed their own children but who, as a result, have the capacity to hold space for the children of others, and for the Mothers of those children, in the moments that they themselves feel close to toppling.

Maybe it would enable us to protect one another – at all stages of life and in all facets of our personality – from the judgement of closed-minded others and the beratings of our imbalanced structures, so that those that stand alongside us and those that will follow us feel safe and supported to challenge those old systems and dynamics. And claim the full power of their own inner sparks once and for all.

And maybe it would remind us of the creative power we have within us to create and gestate the new – be that art, political systems, entirely new theories on the workings of the world or yes, people – when we are not directing all of our creative energy to building a life within someone else's template.

Casting off the constraints of narrow, judgemental Motherhood and instead opening our hearts and minds to the unique power that is Motherhood within us will take courage. But we do not do this alone. Because to reclaim that energy of the Mother is to reclaim the power of connection that we have to one another, to all other Mothers throughout all of time and space. And to remember that we are only the latest in a long line of unthinkably wise, ferociously courageous and giant-heartedly loving women, who were and always have been Mothers.

And who claimed that title for themselves, not because of their personal circumstances, not through their relationships to other people, and not because someone else deemed them to be worthy of it.

But because they shouldered the heartache of watching others suffering across the planet and longed for a way to gather those others up and embrace the whole of humanity, as they fended off threat and harm.

Because they felt the pulse of connection and resonance in their hearts and their wombs, when they placed their hands upon the Earth and joined the dance of the planet, as she claimed them as one of her own.

Because they recognised the sense of joy, beauty and sheer power that exploded within them when they conceived of something new. And embraced both the buzz of energy and love that came with thoughts of tending that newness into being *and* the sheer terror of what it would be if they weren't able to keep this new creation safe.

And because they heard the whisper of a powerful energy within themselves that seemed just one word. One word that reminds us of who we are, what we are capable of, and what has always been within us – just waiting to be honoured and set free.

Mother.

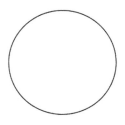

I NEVER SET OUT
TO BE A SPACE HOLDER

By Kathy Bell

space
Noun
A continuous area or expanse which is free, available, or unoccupied.

holder
Noun
A person that holds something.

First off, Dear Reader, I want to set the tone for the term 'space holder.' For me, it's a term I use all the time and know exactly what it means, but it wasn't always this way. The first time I heard it, I was desperately trying to impress some very well-versed space holding people, so that they would give me a job. And the second I heard it, my imagination painted this hilarious image of someone holding air. My inner eyes rolled.

But as they went on to explain the intricacies, complexities and nuances of space holding, I realised it's what I was doing right there at home; as a Mother and a wife:–

It was me trying not to control the outcome but also holding the 'space' for the best outcome to materialise for me and my family.

It was allowing my daughter to make mistakes, and being there for her when she did, with grace, love and genuine understanding.

It was being neutral, loving, forgiving and compassionate (as was humanly possible) as my husband navigated depression.

It was sending deep waves of trust into the life of my baby girl – having faith in her that she would figure it all out separately from me.

It was leaning back and giving my husband space to heal his inner demons, grief and anxiety...no matter what that looked like.

And so much more...albeit not quite as perfectly as I describe here!

Holding space isn't just holding a bit of air. It's the very bones of Motherhood – womanhood.

We are not only the creators, but the compassionate, loving, forgiving nurturers of the world and our loving spaces are what will heal the world. I just know it.

I hope this chapter helps you to see just how important you are as you: Wake Up Mother!

The Journey to this Point

I'll start off by saying there was a lot of resistance to writing this chapter. Even though I absolutely loved the idea. I loved what Sarah was creating and it excited me beyond belief. I was resistant; I missed the calls, I missed the deadline, I muted WhatsApp.

But still, there was a pull; I knew I had to be involved but this underlying magnetic pull felt too much to lean into fully; the truth was I didn't feel worthy of being in the space.

What did I know about being a Mother? (*I've only got one child after all!*)

What did I have to contribute? (*I've avoided all my 'Mother Wounds'!*)

What would it bring up, if I started speaking about my journey of Motherhood? (*Filled with heartbreak, sadness, shame and judgement*).

What shadows would I have to face? (*Oh no, not more!*)

I was resistant, but I kept hearing the title for my chapter: 'I Never Set Out to Be a Space Holder.' And although it sometimes went quiet, it would come back to tap me on the shoulder and give me the nudge to start writing. So, deep in the glorious August heatwave of 2022, I started to write, even though I had missed the deadline, this story oozing out of me, regardless!

Turns out – I hadn't missed the deadline after all. And so by the grace of resistance and writing it anyway; here I am.

What Does it Mean to Be a Mother?

I didn't dream of being a Mother from a young age.

I didn't have toy babies, or prams. I simply wasn't that bothered. My childhood was spent creating 'things' other than a pretend home and a nice place for my toy baby to sleep (like my daughter does).

I'd spend hours in my bedroom drawing, painting, colouring, sticking, cutting; creating. Sure I had Barbies, but I wasn't Mothering them.

I wasn't even that fussed about real babies. I much preferred to *be* the baby actually; the youngest cousin on both sides of my family, the youngest grandchild, the only child.

I loved being taken care of, Mothered, doted on and I loved receiving a Mother's (aunts, Grandmothers, god parents) love.

It wasn't until I turned 27 with a partner who was nine years older than me, that my ovaries started to twitch.

Getting pregnant didn't come easy but it happened, and on my 28th birthday, June 2011, I found out we were expecting a baby girl at our 20 week scan. Both parents were overjoyed.

Winter came and so did our baby. My birth experience was incredible; arriving at the hospital already 5cm dilated (I know), the birth pool was free and I hopped in soon after being examined and enjoyed an easy-ish labour.

(See, I told you I didn't have much wisdom, I even had an easy birth!!)

But what did happen as she was born was something quite extraordinary.

As she passed through my birth canal and into the warm water awaiting her, I felt a bolt of light shoot through my crown chakra and out through my root. I experienced an awakening flash moment as she crowned just before 9pm on the 28th December 2011.

Something BIG shifted. I was no longer the same person. Something changed and I awakened to the mystery that had always been there within me: the mystery that lay dormant waiting for me to remember.

The mystery that I believe is in all of us.

In hindsight, this awakening HAD to happen to ensure I could navigate the next big thing that was on its way. Our daughter's arrival was the preparation, the initiation.

And that big thing led to this *I Never Set Out to Be a Space Holder* title.

But I digress, Dear Reader – this bit is meant to be about what I have learned about what it means to be a Mother.

And so, it was one evening deep in the bedtime routine of our daughter, Iggle Piggle on the TV, husband warming up the milk, that I suddenly realised – this baby that we had brought into the world, wasn't going to be a baby forever.

I had a real 'dogs aren't just for Christmas' moment, except it wasn't a dog, it was a real, live human.

And in that moment I realised being a Mother wasn't just about getting pregnant, having a birth and having a baby – it was SO. MUCH. MORE. And there was no way of being able to know what was to come, or how to navigate it.

And that moment sticks out, because it was the moment I realised my life had changed forever and I couldn't do anything about it.

And since that moment, I've found even deeper meaning to what Mothering is and isn't.

It isn't just about being someone's Mum, cooking their tea, washing (oh endless washing), school trips and untidy bedrooms.

It's actually deep space holding for the Grace of God to move through a physical but spiritual 'thing' in the very human real world.

And by that I'm opening up space for Mothering not only to be about having a baby but also birthing ideas, creations and businesses.

It's about not having the answers, or knowing all the steps. It's about having the courage, compassion, patience and love to hold space for 'something' that ultimately is LOVE itself, as it navigates its way through amnesia to eventual remembering in its own way...no matter what that looks like to you or anyone else for that matter.

Mothering to me, IS the deepest of space holding. It's the deepest form of surrender. It's the most exquisite ride...as you learn that really being a Mother is being a space holder. And if you're clinging, gripping or trying to control it, I want you to know: *you don't have to do that anymore.*

Mothering isn't just for physical Mothers that have birthed a child. Every single woman is here to rebirth the Divine Feminine wisdom that flows through each of us. And we have the capacity to change the world through our magical space holding powers...as I am sure you will read about in other chapters too.

So stay with me, because you're really important...and I want to show you.

I Never Set Out to Be a Space Holder

I've alluded to something 'big' happening during my daughter's early years (the 'thing' that the lightning bolt was preparing me for).

And that, Dear One, occurred on the 28th February 2012.

On the 27th, the night before, I was putting our daughter to bed in her cot when I felt a cold presence at the door. It shuffled in in a familiar way, apologising, it didn't stay long; a quick 'bye' and it was gone.

And I know this sounds weird; for a cold presence to have such a personality, but it truly did.

The next day I got the phone call. My father-in-law had passed away the night before in his sleep.

He had come to say goodbye the night before. He was the cold presence.

I was a naive 28 year old, with a two month old baby and little experience of grief but many, many preconceived, Instagram-influenced ideas about what having a new baby was all about and what that was going to look like.

In reality: I had NO idea what was to come. My expectation was everyone in the family would be sad for a bit, but then come back to the joy of the newest addition to the family and she would get all the love, attention and support that she was destined for. We would do all the things, be the perfect little threesome, maybe even have some more.

What I didn't expect was the unravelling of my husband's mental health or the unravelling of my life as I knew it.

Not only did I have to grieve for my father-in-law and my husband's presence, as he navigated a long depression that included grieving his Mother, too, who had passed away five years previously. There was 'old Kathy' to let go of, and completely abandon what I expected my 4th trimester and my daughter's early childhood to be like.

The joyous first Easter.

Our first family holiday.

Birthday parties, getting ready for Christmas, family gatherings.

Sunday snuggles on the sofa and lazy weekend mornings all huddled together, eating toast.

The first few trips out in the pushchair...

All tainted.

This rupture moment, losing my father-in-law, became the next decade of my life. And it took me on a journey that I now realise is more than worthy of a place at this table because it led me to truly understand what it means to be Mother, a space holder and a bringer of feminine wisdom to Earth.

So back we go to the lightning bolt moment in the birth pool, as my daughter entered the human realm. I said this HAD to happen to prepare me for what was to come didn't I? And I wasn't wrong.

This lightning bolt awakening reminded me of the spiritual connection I had as a child. It stirred this magic inside of me and reminded me I was fucking powerful. It awakened a remembrance and opened me up to spiritual truths that would come to be the vital pillars of support I leaned on, as my life as I knew it started to crumble around me.

As the bolt came through me, I heard the words:

"You've got to stand up. You've got to be all that you're destined to be. You've got to do it for her."

Powerful, but mysterious. I had NO idea.

My hubby took a slow decline into anxiety and depression. Of course – losing both parents before you're even 45 does that kind of thing to people.

Him not being able to engage with us emotionally, physically or mentally was downright terrifying and one of the hardest parts of the past 10 years. The once caring, doting, energetic man I knew, slowly started to slip away and I was alone.

Literally left holding the baby.

And so it was to the spiritual world that I retreated. Of course I had friends, family and my own Mother, but everyone had their own lives: they weren't with me 24/7 but my spirituality could be.

So I started leaning on angels for support.

I started using healing modalities like EFT and Bush Flowers, I even hired my first mentor.

I went down the path of gratitude, mindset work and personal development, praying and setting altars and attuning to the moon – all which seem quite whimsical right now, but they were literally the things that saved me.

I will never apologise for following the call to step into this world and work.

I will never apologise for remembering.

I also found breathwork – which if you know me, you'll know it became a rather large part of my life.

Long story short: Life had thrown me this huge curveball and through it, I realised my superpowers of being a space holder.

I realised what it means to be a Mother, a woman, and lived as a bearer of the mysteries.

This decade of my life was the hardest, darkest and most transformative. And yet it led me to be the very person I needed to be, to do my soul's work and the pillar of light I came to be.

And it isn't just for me. It's not just my work.

This decade brought forward my Divine Feminine wisdom and Divine principles that we all have the capacity, no, DUTY, to access.

Principles I can bet you have also had to develop in your Motherhood journey, because like I said, it's not just my work, this is your work too...

Compassion – had I not been to the depths (more than once) and experienced my own period of depression, I would not be able to hold powerful spaces for my clients, friends, daughter, husband. The depth of empathy, warmth, sensitivity that I have now, just wasn't there before and the world benefits just by having me in it, able to hold this level of compassion. Before this period of my life, I wasn't compassionate... I was selfish and living in my ego.

What's your relationship with compassion? What has happened in your Motherhood journey for you to deepen your level of compassion?

Just remember: the world is a better place because you have a deeper level of compassion.

Forgiveness – I hate to admit it, but I blamed my father-in-law for this period of my life that at times, felt so dark and lonely I could have walked away and never come back. I also felt so angry sometimes I would also cast blame on my husband.

I had to forgive them both. I had to make peace with myself too. Not to mention everyone else who was less than supportive.

Had I not been through this, I'd still be carrying resentment and anger for the guy who cut me up on the slip road last Tuesday. I'd be one walking, talking ball of anger. But I'm able to forgive; quickly, easily and with grace

The world is a better place because I had something and someone to truly forgive. Before this, forgiveness came through forgetfulness.

How about you? Are you clinging or holding onto something that's in the past? Are you holding the hurt? And what if you could 'let it go'? What would that create space for? Who or what have you forgiven?

Understanding – which could similarly be 'kindness.' For me, they go hand in hand. I'm kinder because I'm understanding. I'm understanding because I'm kinder. I understand that people don't always do what you expect them to. I understand that things don't always go the way they're supposed to. I'm not only kinder to myself because of this, but also kinder to others. I've learned that people are complex, unique, wildly varied and yet with a little kindness and understanding - we can move mountains, come together and heal the world.

The moment I allowed my heart to be a little softer and kinder, and allowed myself to try and understand what my husband could be going through, my heart cracked open and light came flooding in.

And we started our long road of recovery and rebuilding our relationship, marriage and partnership as parents.

The world is a better place because I am softer, kinder, understanding, because before this I was dismissive, blunt, negative.

How about you? How has Motherhood allowed you to be more understanding? Kinder? Softer?

Letting Go and Surrender – Aged 28, with a newborn baby – having had nine months to plan, imagine, dream and think about what my early Motherhood journey would look like – suddenly it came crashing down.

I knew nothing.

Nothing.

And that was the point. Some people don't learn the way I did. But we all have those moments where the universe goes: "Nope, you don't know anything, let go..."

And we are forced to let go of the gripping, the micro-managing, the planning. Now this is a lifelong practice for me, but at least I have the experience of deep surrender. And if I can let go of what I thought my first year being a Mother was going to be like, I can let go of anything, right?

Well, I certainly try. Letting go of expectations (for the most part!) has freed me up to be a better human. I'm more grateful for the moment, I'm surprised and delighted by the little things...

And I bet you are too...the world is a better place because we can let go and step into the flow of where life is taking us, rather than constantly trying to control.

Space holding – stepping back and trusting it's all going to work out. Letting go of the gripping and control and leaning back and surrendering to what is. Having and holding deep reverence and respect for another person's journey, not trying to influence or micro-manage – because truly that's what I had to do.

That's what my spiritual journey and this rupture taught me.

That's what the lightning bolt was asking of me.

That's what the words were calling me towards:

"You've got to stand up, you've got to be all that you're destined to be. You've got to do it for her."

It wasn't just the '*her*' I was holding in my arms.

It was for **you** too.

I was asked to go on a journey that would lead me into these principles, these qualities. I was asked to embody more Divine Feminine wisdom and share it. I was asked to write about it, talk about it and walk the path of a human being with all its complexities, pain and darkness. I was asked to not only do it as a Mother but as a wife and partner.

To have this 'story' but be able to see the power of the story and not stay a victim of the story.

Would I change the last 10 years? Well there are certainly parts I'd rather didn't happen, but on the whole; I love my journey. I'm in awe of my soul's commitment to being here and Mothering to these levels. I'm not afraid of the darkness anymore and that is a true gift.

And I want you to know, see, understand just how much of you is also in me – how similar we are. How we all have this capacity for heartache, darkness and pain, and yet can rise and resurrect over and over again – with the grace, love and compassion of an ascended master.

The world is a better place because YOU ARE A SPACE HOLDER.

Thank you.

The world is a better place because YOU MOTHER.

Thank you.

The world is a better place because YOU HAVE BEEN WILLING TO SAY YES TO LIFE.

Thank you.
Thank you.
Thank you.

Together we rise.

THE SECRET PATH TO MOTHERHOOD

By Rachel Haywood

I'd always wanted to be a Mother.

Though I'm not sure those who've known me would have thought that, as having my own life first was just as important to me.

I wanted to explore, discover, have fun, travel – do ALL the things. But as I did this, what I realised – and feared – was that I wasn't actually that suited to having children. I'd always been quite a free spirit, a life-on-my-own terms sort, who also loved the cosiness of cages – providing the door was left wide open.

The reality of Motherhood felt like an entrapment that I doubted I'd ever be ready for. The irony was that unbeknownst to me, I was already incarcerated in more than one invisible cage.

I didn't really think I was 'Mother material' with all that sacrifice, routine and a softness I wasn't sure I possessed. It also looked a lot like having to give up my armour, which had been firmly in place since I was very young, keeping me strongly in control.

It was useful in advocating, protecting the underdog and those less courageous – but most importantly, kept a part of me very well hidden. I'm pretty good at championing other people's things, but not so great at my own. Which is probably why I made quite a good stepmother (I'd like to think my step-kids would agree).

Over the years, lots of things have felt out of reach to me, as I was unable to embrace what felt like weakness and step onto the wobbly bridge of vulnerability........

I needn't have worried at first. There was no conscious choice about it, as the simple act of being pregnant took care of that. Involuntary tears are quite common in my family, but it was not a trait that I ever held. The surprise and horror of not being able to control my emotions was shocking and amusing in equal parts. Little did I know that this was an irrevocable change in the direction of my life and nothing would ever be the same again. Not that I realised at first, or for quite a while after. It's a shift that is subtle, till you glance backward one day and realise the enormity of what has changed. You really do need the full range for such an undertaking. And I use that exact word, because there is a part of you that's lost forever when you have total responsibility for another being.

The incredibly secret path to Motherhood has often perplexed me. Then I think back to whether I actually would have listened. What would I say now? Prepare yourself with a spine of steel, but with more surrounding softness than you've ever known? Be prepared to cry more as a Mother than you ever did as a child? Feel more love than you ever did before? Don't expect any of it to pan out how you imagined? Be prepared to take the most crazy, intense, emotional trip of your life? Be prepared to lose all control and exist suspended in an altered state forever?

It sounds a little dramatic in all honesty. And thinking back to how we structure the preparation to such an event, do we even know what we're in for? I'd initially planned to work right up to the date as I was being made redundant. Then with about three weeks to go, I was suddenly hit by the magnitude of what was about to happen and needed some time and space to process it all. Without any competition for my mental capacity.

There was (and continues to be) so much I hadn't bargained for. After the care and consideration leading up to the 20-week scan, the daddy ended up taking a job out of town. This was after a lull in work prospects following a period of house renovation, me finishing a project, Christmas, and my now looming redundancy. What was supposed to be our last summer as a twosome, was nothing of the sort. It really, probably was the beginning of the end.

They say three is a crowd, but we'd managed being a four every other weekend when the step kids came to stay.....

I'd also mistakenly thought that having a baby would be a great way to integrate into a new place where I knew no-one. I'd loved hanging out with my friends on their maternity leave and was looking forward to having that sort of fun. We'd left London to be closer to the big kids and having a baby was part of the deal. Being left on my own in our rural house while the daddy worked away during the week was not.

Thankfully, I had my parents for the first six weeks, but that was awkward during the weekends. And the influx of sisters and families, and a friend who surprised me from the other side of the world, just added to the already complicated pot.

Looking back, there were moments of absolute joy before the loneliness set in. My family first arriving was so special. Here I was finally celebrating my own occasion instead of what felt like a Lifetime of other people's. My Mother commented on what a relaxed first-time Mother I was, which was true, it did feel rather peaceful in the very beginning. It was summer and I'd imagined sunny days of lounging around in the garden having the best, most precious time of my life. The reality was it was possibly quite a grey summer, our house never had an indoor/outdoor flow in those days, and the inside of the house was dark. It didn't help that the daddy wasn't integrating with any sort of gratitude during the weekends towards the people who were keeping me afloat. It turned out having a new baby is bewildering to say the least.

Then my family all went home and I was truly alone with a tiny baby in the middle of nowhere. I loved every stage of those early months as a Mother, but I was so lonely, bereft and miserable as a person. Then of course I felt awful for my precious boy that he had such a sad Mother. My saving grace was having insisted on the NCT course where I could buy myself some friends. Those girls, baby yoga and the postnatal group at the local town were the only touch points where I could keep my sanity and connection. The strange thing was that when we first moved up here, I didn't miss having people around at all. It was so exciting to be embarking on my own journey of homeownership, my own garden and a commute that left little time for anything else. We got a dog and a whole lot more cats. We also planned a wedding, got married and had a lot of visitors....... But the minute I became a Mother, I've never needed people so much – and they just weren't around. I was so out of my depth. I've never felt so far from myself. Though that took a while to register.

My biggest advice at this point is make sure you have support.

Do not have a baby on your own without a support system.
Just don't. Ever.

And the worst of it was, I was now drowning in what felt like weakness, making it even harder to know how to step onto the wobbly bridge of vulnerability and ask for help. And to who?

Please make sure you have people around who know you, and knew you before you had a baby and your identity fell out. I know people talked to me about being invisible when they had babies, but I could never really fathom what they meant. I could still see them clearly?

Then it happens to you, and you don't even notice at first – until everyone gets back to their lives. It's also really hard to make new friends by connecting with like people, when there's nothing left of your similarity to reflect back at them.

The thing is, I thought I'd prepared quite well. I'd specifically asked the NCT breastfeeding woman what happens when you can't, which surprisingly appeared to be a question she couldn't answer. So I'd chosen my Health Visitor to help me through that hurdle, given the fact I hardly ever saw the same midwife twice. It was a classic project management approach – identify the risks and mitigate. I'd arranged 'hyper-care' in the form of parents, but no-one had pointed out the need for training, an ongoing support provision, or a change management plan to ensure the project would be successful. Everything at that point had been planned around the main 'Go Live' event – but that was one day (OK a few in my case) and then of course, once you're 'on the other side' there is absolutely no space or capacity for sensible planning.

One of the biggest problems I had was no edges. Being made redundant while I was pregnant meant there was no set timeframe. No closed container. Just an open-ended window of fairly lonely daily repetitions. The fact that they'd offered me my job back while I was in hospital with a newborn baby infuriates me now. This in response to legal action (they were reinstating the department after all and those not having babies – ie a male colleague – would probably have their redundancy revoked). Not only could I not think properly, but getting on a train to Canary Wharf where the office had moved to was incomprehensible. No-one had conveyed what it would physically feel like to contemplate not being near your baby. And no-one told me what it would feel like to have a baby and not be near your friends or family....

Near the end of the first six months, we were able to plan a trip home to NZ which was a welcome relief from pressured weekends of a grumpy dad, sulky teenagers and a crying baby. No-one seemed to be sharing in the joy of him, just all resenting the effect he had on the whole household. Having had a week of calm, the tension changed the minute the daddy walked through the door and we all ducked under the parapet. Which was not an easy place to keep a baby quiet.

New Zealand was a dream. It was brilliant to eventually be home, surrounded by all my friends and family, sharing the joy of Motherhood, which felt surprisingly easy when I felt most myself and completely supported.

Mum had often reminded me that Gran said, 'Babies bring their own joy,' and finally I could feel what she meant. The universe cast some star alignment and we even had a spontaneous second wedding, gathering friends from far and wild, with two weeks' notice. But we had to come back 'home' to reality, and what a trip that turned out to be. The reality, not the journey home.

It's the decision making that comes with Motherhood which I find the hardest. Every minute of every day and the continuous assessment of the knock on effects. They say that Mothers know their children best and what is best for them. But I didn't. I made some terrible choices around childcare. Which confused me and sent me further away from trusting myself. I felt strongly about my instincts in the beginning, but not having people I knew and trusted around to bounce ideas off was really difficult. They also say that Mothers know when things aren't right. I shudder to look back now at the utter shock, disbelief, isolation, worry – and I think I'll add in shame here – that there might have been something 'wrong' with my child.

I think we did the usual things at this point with a hearing test, speech drop-in and a follow up to the 2-year check, which of course took months of waiting.

Life was busy in other ways with a new job, family visiting, then the flatlining of winter.

The latter which ended up in the implosion of our marriage and the sudden escalation of my son's behaviour.

What followed was a long path of assessment, but the incidents were so closely correlated with what was going on at home, it didn't necessarily feel true to me. Then having the surprise NHS diagnosis completely out of the blue just threw me even further. Then the incompetence surrounding the lack of requested follow up, genetic testing and the private diagnostic report, further again.

None of this has been easy, but I wish I'd had more support earlier on – known that there were people who are able to provide guidance and mentoring through those first months of establishing myself as a Mother. Who might have been able to help me keep pieces of myself that I'd need.

Having spent the latter years of adulthood trying to grow up and conform, left me completely unprepared for raising a child like mine. Funnily enough an old friend of mine, who knew me years before, thought if anyone could do it, it was me. And despite having a job where my expertise and decisions were valued, I've never felt so clueless and completely at the mercy of all the 'professionals' and their experience.

Not to mention how out of place I felt amongst the cliques of the school playground, where everyone had loads of kids and were ten years younger. While I was cycling through identity shifts with desperation and despair, my little bear was emerging as the most vibrant, energetic and determined force of nature.

There was really no room for my insecurities while escorting my 5-year-old son through school in fairy dresses and (my long discarded) high heeled shoes. When we weren't late, which was most of the time.

I just didn't know who I was anymore, but by the side of my crazy little bear, I couldn't stay moping in my shadows. The spotlight was on and I had to step up.

I was ill-equipped to deal with a lot of it, as I'd been too busy trying to embody all the roles – wife, Mother, employee, leaving no space for myself. But they are just roles – they are not who we are. It's no wonder we lose ourselves in Motherhood, as we've already given ourselves away previously.

Our lives are like a performance, playing all the parts, constant wardrobe changes, and waiting eagerly for the recognition that we've got it right. Always trying to be good enough – but for who? By stepping into these roles, we lose touch with who we really are, which is the cause of such suffering. I wasn't sure who I was without my job. I wasn't sure who I was as a wife. With all my false identities, I wasn't strong enough to figure out who I was as a Mother. Then when all hell broke loose I was fucked.

Whereas all I ever really needed to be was myself. In all of it. He chose me to be his Mother for entirely different reasons as to whether I could meet his needs in the approving eyes of others.

Delving into the issues with his behaviour made me realise how completely unprepared so many of us are for parenting.

Why do we think we'll just know how to be Mothers, because women have been doing it for years? You only need to watch the news or read the paper to see that clearly we're doing something very wrong in how children have been raised to date.

Additional needs support is dressed up as parenting classes, which feels insulting and missing of the point. But what's actually being missed is that everyone needs parenting awareness. More role models of conscious parenting. Support and focus on love and acceptance, instead of fear and judgement. Our children need us to see them and know them, which we can only do by knowing ourselves first. And supporting each other to be those selves, instead of perpetuating the myth of the perfect version of Motherhood.

As we approach his 7th birthday, I realise how far we've come. He is unapologetically himself and has never tried to fit in to anything other than his own desires, with everything preferably in his own time and space. He is completely unconventional, quirky, kind, mischievous, helpful and loving. Because of him, I am returning to me.

He reminds me who I was. Who I've become. Who I am.

That I was never here to follow the rules, adhere to boundaries, or play it safe. I'm tired. But he encourages me to WAKE UP.

Put my armour back on again and get back to advocating, protecting the underdog and those less courageous. But to take it off too. Without hiding parts of myself. Exploring that vulnerability, where it leads, and expanding into my softness.

Being his Mum has opened up a more gentle side of myself that I never felt comfortable in before.

It hasn't been easy – and the path we're on is completely unknown and different to what I ever would have imagined. But it's a joy, an adventure, and an exploration in itself. One that has as many wonders, highs and lows – taking the most extreme opposites of human and divine experience and intrinsically weaving them together into the most extraordinary and miraculous journey of all.

What I've realised is that Mothering is as much as a spectrum as anything else. There is no right way to be a Mother, but many ways. I am also a Mother to cats and a dog. I'm a Stepmother. I'm a Godmother.

But the best Mothers know they don't have to do it alone. The best Mothers know it's best when we all lean in together. And not just Mothers, but all women, young and old. Collectively we all have something to offer to each other at all stages of our beautiful cyclical paths.

MOTHER

By Katherine Crawley

So much is held within this word. So much that has been lost, repressed, controlled, misunderstood.

Mother is the force of life itself. It is sentient in all living things.

It is the Springtime, it is the Autumn, it is the Summer, it is the Winter; Mother is cyclical, Mother is omnipresent, Mother is Home.

But as we have lost a deeper intimate connection with ourselves, as women, we have lost the capacity to resource the true embodied power and wisdom that is Mother.

The society we live in has raped and pillaged this Earth, our Mother, just as the patriarchy has colonised, controlled and silenced women.

We have been severed from the source; severed from a river of creative manifesting life giving energy; severed from ourselves.

As women, we have been hollowed out. We have forgotten our embodied wisdom; we have forgotten what it is to Be Mother.

Mother has become a factory of baby making; isolated, disempowered and deeply disconnected from the natural rhythms of the Earth. The rhythms that are our birthright.

Women are alone and lost, relying so heavily on the patriarchy to explain to them what is happening in their bodies. To tell them what they should be feeling; how they should be managing their periods; how they should be managing their sex lives; how they should be conceiving; how they should be giving birth; how they should be Mothering.

As I dive into this rich material, my heart aches for all women and the deep suffering that ails us.

We are so deeply programmed, through our functional nervous system, to please, to keep the peace, to make sure everyone else is happy – something that society then exploits, so that we very often don't even realise the distortions we are living.

We beat ourselves up, tell ourselves we are not worthy; we should be better, we need to keep a lid on our emotions, we need to think positive, we need to keep going, keep smiling, be nicer, be kinder, until one day, we wake up with a hernia and then five years later, we are diagnosed with a life threatening disease.

The dis-ease that so many women suffer from comes from a lifetime of deep internal conflict with ourselves, as we try to be something we are not, and totally disregard the wisdom and power of who we truly are.

So what is my Mother story? ...

The truth is, after having two sons, one who is 10 and the other who is 4, I am still waking up to truly embodying Mother.

Because what I am understanding, at a deeply felt sense level, i.e. from an experiential right brain place, as opposed to a left brain cognitive place, is that waking up to Mother, is about so much more than having children.

It is really the greatest initiation into feminine embodied wisdom and power that we go through as women, in our lives. And yet our culture, our society, our lineages have lost all true understanding of what that is.

We have so little understanding of the power of our energetic bodies full stop – living our lives in the dis-connection of our rational minds – that it is no wonder that we cannot feel the transformative energetic power of Mother.

And so the journey 'Home' to the deepest essence of who we are, as women, whether we have children or not, is usually a painful one. Painful as we overcome our childhood conditioning, our deep ancestral traumas and our cultural judgments and interpretations.

There is a lot to wade through and there is so little support as we do.

For me, it has been through the journey of bringing new human life to this Earth, that I have opened to this awareness. I have been challenged to the core of me, undone on every level of my identity and dropped into the depths of pain, grief and loss to be slowly birthed and re-birthed again and again into an ever deeper, truer, more authentic expression of Woman, of Mother.

And what that distinction is and whether there actually is one, I will dive into a little later.

First, I am moved to go back to the birth of my first son.

The struggles began during pregnancy, as is so often the case, where my intuition told me one thing and the medical profession told me another.

I had a blissfully happy and healthy pregnancy, practicing yoga twice a week and was excited to birth in the beautiful new birthing centre at Paddington Hospital in London.

Everything then changed when I went in for my 40 week check-up and was told that I had low blood platelets, was high risk and would hence need to give birth on the main ward of the hospital, after all.

I do not have a happy relationship with hospitals. Sadly across my life I have had numerous traumatic experiences, in the hands of heavy handed and inconsiderate doctors.

But I think the deep mistrust comes from my pre-cognitive infantile experience of being separated from my Mother, hours after birth, and left screaming in a glass crib, far away from any warm body or regular heartbeat.

Oh, and then my first smear test at 13 years old, lying on my back, legs spread with a cold metal contraption stuck up inside me, as I watched it all in the reflection of the photograph on the ceiling, was definitely another deeply traumatising one.

So being delivered this news at 40 weeks pregnant, put me in a deep state of panic. I felt totally trapped and afraid.

We considered home birth, but my husband felt really uncomfortable about that, out of fear for my health, he said, but in hindsight, I feel, it was out of fear of the unknown.

And so with the amazing support of our doula, we agreed to work within the hospital system and push for the water birth, I had dreamed of.

I will not go into all the traumatic details, but should probably mention the nurse's words to me on the ward: "It's not the journey of how you get there that matters, it's the destination!"

Wow that just all felt so wrong that I then spent the next five hours in a dark bathroom, trying to find my safe place in which to bring my baby into the world.

It brings tears to my eyes as I write, remembering how un-nurtured I felt. Thank God I had my doula with me the whole time. She was absolutely amazing, as I squatted down during contractions, in the corner of the dark bathroom, holding onto a scarf wrapped around her waist.

I will never forget that bright pink Mexican scarf!

I am really taken aback by how much grief there still is, as I relive this now. I remember, Jessie, my doula, saying to me that it takes a lifetime to get over birth trauma – she wasn't wrong. But hopefully this book will inspire women to be more open with allowing their deeper feelings, fears, regrets and pain to be heard.

Because this is where we are so severed from our true wisdom and resilience. So conditioned to silence our feelings and repress our emotions, we lose ourselves, our true identities, the heartbeat of our souls.

So after hanging in there for 42 weeks and two days, in a body that felt too unsafe to give birth, my baby boy was born into a birthing pool, at around 5pm on December the 29th, 2011.

He swam out and then nestled onto my chest for a few moments before being taken away from me and given to his father, whilst I was stitched up.

I can still feel the deep pain of that unnatural separation. I had carried him for nine months, had just gone through a both traumatic and empowering birth and now he was gone.

My body was screaming for him, my whole system on red alert. How little we understand these natural processes ... no wonder I then suffered from high blood pressure.

And so that was the beginning of my becoming a biological Mother.

I had been lucky that my Mother was a very progressive spiritual woman, who had handed me the 8th edition of *The Art of Breastfeeding* during my pregnancy and so I felt like I had some idea of what I was doing with the 'skin-to-skin' and then allowing my little bundle of love to snuffle his way naturally, to the breast.

It was a blissful experience, which I know is so very different for each of us.

I remember being in the ward, full of screaming babies, which was totally traumatic. Bode, my son, was still mostly naked on my chest, mostly peaceful, whilst so many babies were in their glass cribs next to the beds, alone, often crying.

My challenge was trying to go to the loo because I didn't want to leave him on his own.

The first time I managed to take him with me, but I had a great big pad on and was bleeding quite heavily. It was crazy and the feeling of being so alone, after my partner had to go home and my sister had just left back to Mexico, came in big tears pouring down my cheeks.

Eventually one of the nurses came quite sternly, to tell me that I needed to put some clothes on him and put him down, so we could both get some rest.

We were all new mums grappling with finding our way in an environment that is, through default, deeply un-nurturing.

We mostly have no idea what we're doing and for the first time in our lives, we're trying to tune into our intuitive wisdom.

We've forever been told how to look after our feminine bodies, how to regulate our hormones, how to exercise birth control, how to have the best orgasms. We've been told how to do everything and so it's little wonder that, all of a sudden, as we are expected to just 'be a mum,' we feel totally lost and drowning.

It's what we were designed to do, so surely we should just be able to do it!

Not when we have been so deeply disempowered our whole lives, trying to fit into a deeply dysfunctional patriarchal world, where our sensitivities are seen as weaknesses and our emotions as something that need to be regulated.

Our menstrual cycles are judged a pain in the proverbial, something to get over, to control, to overcome.

It always blows me away that our relationship with our periods is still so deeply dysfunctional, when there would be no life on Earth, if we women didn't bleed every month.

But of course, because this is really part of our greatest power, the patriarchy has repressed it and demonised it.

So this is why, it is my deep belief and embodied experience that the deep disconnection from our Mother Energy and wisdom begins when we step through menarche.

This should be a time of sacred initiation for us – a coming into the creative cycles of our lives, as we awaken to our feminine pleasure and cyclical wisdom.

The coming of our blood is a gift, a rite of passage into womanhood.

But where are the women's circles to hold us as we step forward?

Where is our Mother's, our Grandmother's wisdom to guide us through?

Where is our sisterhood to welcome us with open loving arms?

It's been buried and then forgotten because it had to be, in order to survive.

Remember, they used to burn medicine women, midwives, Crones...

Ooh the anger bubbles up – how we have been repressed, silenced, disempowered, disembodied.

So it's really from the moment we start to bleed that we're on the back foot, that instead of celebrating and enjoying our feminine bodies and our embodied wisdom and power, which would then guide us smoothly into Motherhood, we're just grappling to find some kind of acceptable identity that fits into what society tells us we need to be.

We need to be a good girl, we need to be a pretty girl, we need to be accomplished, kind, smart, caring, hard-working, a good girlfriend, a good lover, a good wife, a good Mother ....

How the f**k are we supposed to know how to be a good Mother!!??

So although I was blessed to be able to hear my intuitive Mothering wisdom coming through – almost three decades of being a yogi meant I had access to my inner sensory awareness system – the environment in which I found myself didn't seem to align with it, in any way.

Luckily, we only lived a 15 minute walk from the hospital and so I could walk my son home in a sling, as there was no way my intuition was going to put my two day old child in a car seat in the back of the car.

He then stayed in that sling for almost two years really!

I know attachment parenting is not for everyone and that's OK, but for me it made total sense to have my son next to my heart, listening to my heart beat, as he did in the womb, feeling my breath coming in and out of my lungs and breathing the same air I breathed, as opposed to the toxic fumes of the London traffic, in a pram that would have put him at exhaust emission level.

But I was certainly the odd one out in Notting Hill, where we lived – no Bugaboo pram, no sleep training, no bottle feeding.

For some reason, well because of all that I have shared really, about how deeply lost we are to ourselves, we judge others that don't fit in with our chosen ways.

I was guilty of that too. It was like a lion's den as opposed to a sisterhood circle around Portobello Market.

And so I used to walk 1 hr 30 mins through the park, north, up to Kentish Town, to go to a Mums and Baby Group, once a week, with Mothers that were more aligned with my approach.

I longed to be able to share stories, to talk openly with others, without feeling judged, without judging, in all my vulnerability.

And that felt like a more nurturing space for me, although I still worried that I didn't belong, because we don't know where we belong really.

Until we belong within ourselves, we mostly have no clue who we truly are. We have no deep connection to our feminine souls.

We are women on the outside, desperately searching for how to be Women/Mothers on the inside.

And I was having to fight tooth and nail to let my Mothering instincts be heard, to let my true inner voice be the guide. To my husband, it was all so un-aligned with what he knew and to what his Mother made very clear, she believed to be right.

And of course, because I felt so alone, so threatened, unheard and unseen, my energy was pretty toxic and so our son, Bode, suffered from terrible colic for his whole first year of life. It was sleep deprivation hell.

And it's only after years of contemplation and research, that I have come to understand that it was caused by a mixture of the deep anxiety he picked up on from me, in the final weeks of pregnancy and then all the stress and fear that was coming through my body and milk during those first three months.

From that perspective, maybe having him in his own cot, in his own room, would have saved him from all that, but that wasn't our story.

Our story was to find our voice, was to go against the old fashioned upper middle class ways that we were steeped in and to lovingly and often desperately show that picking up our baby when he cried or nursing him to sleep, as well as co-sleeping, was all perfectly acceptable!

One of the big arguments against it, I used to hear, was that our marriage would suffer.

Well I smile deviously in the face of that today, with our four year-old still co-sleeping with us, we have the best sex life we've had in our lives!

So I spent the early years of Motherhood grappling around, having lots of quite violent arguments with my husband, trying to make myself heard, trying to align myself to what I knew to be right. I was fraught, I was just surviving, I was alone.

Then about five years ago, when I suffered a miscarriage, trying for our second child, a deeper shift took place in me.

I was kneeling on the banks of a river in Scotland, where we lived, bleeding into the waters, when I felt this deep awareness, of being in my feminine body, arise in me.

All of a sudden I could really feel my womb and in feeling the deepest places within my body, I could feel the presence of Mother.

Mother Earth, Mother of all life was not only holding me in that moment, but she was moving through me. As if the river was flowing through me, I was coming alive in a way I hadn't been in my whole life.

I was awakening to Mother. Oh how I wept ...

And this shifted everything for me. I went into a period of grieving for the life I had lost, but almost more importantly, for all the years of deep disconnection from my embodied self, that I had lived.

I then embarked on my path of womb healing and women's awakening and sat humbly with the guilt and shame of how I had used and abused my body for so many years, as an object of desire, without any real understanding of her sacred power and wisdom.

Goddess, which I now know as the feminine source of all life, was tingling within me. It truly was like being born again.

And so my next pregnancy and birth were a gift, that in many ways, the woman I had been, could have never imagined possible.

On the night of a red full moon, my second son was danced into the world in our little cottage by the sea in Scotland, my husband by my side and my Mother and eldest son, in the other room.

It was heaven and I had worked hard at it, in deep meditation and yoga every single day, cultivating the flow of Shakti energy, Mother Energy flowing through me. Because in this way, my intuitive wisdom was more grounded, more potent, more full of love than any doubts of medical conditions that were thrown at me.

And much was advised – I was what they called a 'geriatric Mother' for goodness sake! But I lovingly ignored it all, because Mother was guiding me and in her arms, I knew deep in my soul, that I was safe.

And that remains the daily practice, to spend time aligning with our internal compass, our own embodied truth, what we feel at a soul level, to be right.

This is different to fear-driven instincts. This is about deeply grounded, felt sense awareness. It comes from a place of sensitivity and alignment within. It is womb centred, as well as heart centred. It is whole and it is holistic.

And so when it comes to giving our children the best possible start in life, my sense is that a total reframing needs to take place.

We are conditioned to prepare them for a highly competitive, isolating world, where the focus is all on external pursuits and achievements. But this is not where our deepest resources lie. They lie within us, in the fabric of our beings, in our hearts, in our intuitive wisdom, in our reverence for Mother.

Every day is a challenge to find a balance between the pulls of 'doing' and the deeper calling of sensitising, listening and 'being.'

It was through the undoing of my body, that my greatest love and embodied power came to me. And in that place, I know that I am no longer ever, alone.

I walk barefoot in the grass and lie belly down on the Earth, often naked, womb to womb, daily, as I allow myself to be infused with Mother.

And it's from that place that I then endeavour to show up in the world, to be of service to humanity, to Mother my two boys and to share my life with my husband.

And when I am truly aligned there is so little 'doing' that takes place, because the potency of 'being' is so strong that things just fall into place and align.

The language of Mother is love. Not objective/subjective love, but boundless unconditional embodied love. It is the gift of every breath you take, deliciously and sensually into your feminine temple, your body.

The altar of Mother is within your womb and you hold the keys to unleashing Her wisdom and majesty.

The Dalai Lama said that the hope for creating sustainable life on Earth, lies in the re-awakening of women in the West.

Mother, our Earth, our Home needs us to remember that we are Her and She is us.

And so let go of your to-do lists, tell your critics and judges to F-off and start breathing more deeply deep down into your womb. Re-sensitise your body. Remember that she is a powerful temple, receiving and perceiving the energies of the world around her.

Shake, dance, breathe, scream, laugh and then shake some more and THEN sit quietly and listen within ... it's all there and this is my loving call to support you, to remember.

And....

Let's be really kind with ourselves and never forget that we are highly hormonal creatures, that we have generations of caged wild animal trauma to overcome and so a lot of the time, it's all really, really messy.

Tired, exhausted, stretched, fraught, unheard, unseen, unappreciated, desperate are all part of this journey, and mostly states into which we put ourselves because we are so deeply trained to keep going, to keep doing. Despite it all, we will keep caring, keep nurturing, keep putting our children, our partners, everyone before ourselves.

I fall into the martyr persona, a powerful self-sacrificing martyr and often observe myself from the outside in, doing the laundry, cooking the meals with everyone's different dietary requirements, doing bath time, reading stories, putting the boys to bed, cleaning up the kitchen and, and, and ... pushing, pushing, pushing in this manic survival mode, often just too exhausted to know how to stop!

And then I'm angry deep down inside that there's no-one to help me. But the truth is I don't know how to help myself.

So go gently, really gently, stop pushing. Don't push from one modus operandi to another modus operandi, there is no wisdom in that.

It's more about getting to know the martyr, because she's been an amazing survivor for many years and many lifetimes. And without her you wouldn't have survived, had a roof over your head, food to eat.

Somewhere in your not so distant past, your survival personality is what kept you alive and it may not have been a very good life, you might have been verbally abused, you might have been beaten, you might even have been sexually abused, but you were alive and that was enough.

But times have changed and although our central nervous systems don't often realise that yet, we can say no and not get beaten anymore. We can walk away and not be in risk for our lives.

We have choices now, in the West.

Because not all women do. But I do and if you're reading this book, you probably do too.

You have a choice as to whether you continue to perpetuate the ancestral subservient, people pleasing, victim-steeped, martyr strong personality, or not.

You have the key to the cage that your past has put you in.

And in the softness and tenderness, in the forgiveness and compassion; in the love, the unconditional sacred love for all the amazing woman you are, you can fly free from your cage once more …. Mother.

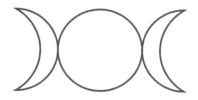

MY MOTHERHOOD:
MY HOMECOMING

By Aimee Strongman

Motherhood is messy
Motherhood is raw
This Motherhood is mine
And my Motherhood is pure.

One woman's connection to her Mother Energy and how she found her soul purpose as a Mother, and voyaged into this realm without a map or compass. Mothering is wild, ungracious and unforgiving at times and can feel like the whole world sees you bare. But it can also unlock the truest parts of yourself, spark the Mother fire in your belly and guide you to your village.

As I begin to think about how best to share my wisdom with you, I realise that this story is just one thread of many beautiful and unique, wild, light and dark yarns, woven throughout time into a colourful and rich tapestry on the loom of 'Mother.' It is a universal path and rite of passage that our society has overlooked, undervalued and misunderstood.

I know for some 'Mother' may be the steppingstone from Maiden to Mother and into this undulating seascape of Mothering children, or it may be the portal of birthing a business, a project or simply a rebirth into something new and an exciting beginning. It may resonate with you as the birth of a book, a piece of creative art or a successful endeavour. But whatever we give birth to, we are returning. Returning to wisdom that is held in our bones and locked within the very core of each of us.

In 'Mothering' there is a deep process that happens. Like the turning of the seasons. An inexplicable trust and knowing that there is a rhythm to follow and honour. Like the budding of a rose in Spring, we witness our coming of age and then we bloom. We stand in our fullness in our summer season, beautiful with rich abundance and activity. In this season of womanhood, we are alive in 'Mother' – this lifeforce cascading through every part of our being, awakening us to the wisdom we hold. It is the bass beat that you hear, at the heart of your soul, your truest essence, existing so deep in the wellspring of your womb or womb space, just below your navel. It is like all cyclical things in life, constant yet changing, as time moves forward. And as you bathe in this light, glowing in full sovereignty and reflect on the journey here, you stand in the realisation that you are exactly where you are supposed to be. A pregnant pause before we experience again another shift into a different realm; into the season of the wild woman, as we approach menopause, and then the wise woman, the enchantress, Grandmother elder.

My Grandmother's name was Joy and even now when I see the word I smile. Joy; a Grandmother, Mother, sister, midwife and a woman who helped others. She was a maternal figure in the community and worked in the NHS until she was 72. I lived with her and my grandfather from the age of 21. She was my home. When I write the word 'home,' to me it is a word that encompasses many different emotions and feelings, enclosed in a safe space filled with love, understanding and safety. I went away to school at the age of seven and when I was eight, my family circumstances changed. My parents divorced and I lived with my father. He was in the military at the time, so it was not unusual for us to be on the move and creating home in different houses. I think I've always been on a quest to find my own place to call 'home' and a great sense of belonging. My Motherhood is my homecoming.

I lost my Grandmother six months before I got married. I was at the pinnacle of my Maiden voyage, a time of transition and a time to celebrate, but I was missing the one person I wanted to share it with. I wanted to thank her for taking care of me, for looking after me and for really showing me the meaning of Mother Energy. I wanted to share the love that was felt and for her to witness my joy. She was my confidante and the one who knew each archetype of me best of all.

My husband had also lost his father four months before our nuptials so between us we were dealing with a lot of heartache and grief. Yet at the same time, wrapped up and filled with so much love for one another. It was a hard time, and the grief came in waves for us both, but the cycle was evident. The final met with the inaugural; the end and the beginning entwined as one, weaving their way into our future unbeknownst to us.

After a walk through the heather on the heathland, under the Perseid meteor shower one special night in August, just a year after we were married, I gave birth to my firstborn son on the living room floor. It changed my life, shattered my soul and burst my heart wide open.

In an instant I was awakened. I was awake to every sensation, every tingle on my skin, every smell, every sound every little thing that moved. It was as if the vibration of life had been raised and I was feeling it all.

The experiential learning was that childbirth was the most powerful, illuminating and tender happening. It felt to me like an otherworldly experience. I was hovering above, looking down on myself at the threshold between two worlds, watching this baby being born. It felt like an intense force of energy searing through me, and I was witness to it all.

My first thought, on reflecting on my birth experience was, "Why has no-one ever told me I could do this?"

I used my hypnobirthing breathing, peppered with a yogic breath called 'Ujai' and I kept my body moving during pregnancy with yoga and aqua natal classes. But why had no-one ever shared with me the sheer power of a woman? The capabilities of her body? The truth and the physiology of childbirth? I felt incredibly powerful, yet so vulnerable at the same time. It was a sensitive time of meeting a new me and struggling with a new identity and the pace of life shifting so dramatically. No longer was I galivanting to London at weekends to see friends for cocktails and dinner or planning to teach 30 primary school children about connectives and conjunctions. I was at home, just me and my baby. Soft, leaking, fragile and delicate, feeding this gorgeous being on the sofa hour after hour, day in day out, trying to figure it all out.

Each night I was seeking others who might be up like me experiencing this new life.

Thank goodness for the moon and her rhythmic cycles. Many nights I would look to her light and watch the stars, trying to grasp a sense of comfort and grounding. It was a relentless schedule of life-keeping and housekeeping and celebrating the small wins of showering or getting dressed.

I didn't feel like me.

The shadows danced and despite all the support from my family and friends, it was a massive shock to the system. I felt the jarring in my heart, body and mind. These pillars of my entire existence were being knocked and shook with force. This is the power of creation. This is the movement of Motherhood: to rock us and to shock us, but never to stop us. The darkness of the Mother Energy will shake you to the core. But it is in these moments, when shadows cast shade, that glimmers of light can been seen.

Serendipitously, during these early months of my Motherhood, a job came up for my husband. He applied for a job in Dorset (we were living in Kent at the time) in a town I used to know. There were no plans in place, and we had no idea where this new role might lead us. So, with a 5-month-old baby in tow, we found ourselves in a country village in the heart of Dorset with woodland all around and in a place my Grandmother had loved.

Something about this place felt like home and there was a strange sense of calm. It was where I had lived growing up in my teenage years, coincidentally where I came of age, and now I was a new Mother with just the familiarity of a place where I had once lived, which felt bizarrely reassuring. A comfortable feeling of knowing the land yet not the people, mirroring the Motherhood I was deep within, where everything felt uncertain, new, unknown, unexplored.

I immersed myself in Mother Nature and joined a local forest school and slowly began to build a new relationship with myself and the others around me. The 'Great Mother' calling me back to remember the ancient wisdom of our ancestors. In the woods I felt safe, held by the communal Mother Energy; sitting in circle, talking, sharing and watching our babes play and interact with no expectation or judgement. This space and these women became my village gathering every Friday for five years. The woodland was my sanctuary and I felt so connected to the Earth; her smells, her seasons, her energy surrounding every seedling, flower, clearing and tree. I felt watched and cared for by the women, who like me, were in this heart space of Mothering, trying to navigate the waves wanting to feel steady on her shores.

Over time I learned to go slow, to live a softer day. I managed to shake off the 'shoulds' and breathed in more moments of 'wow'. The first exploration of the woodland in winter, the sightings of bluebells in the clearing, the smell of the wild garlic and chatter about what we would be making with nature's offerings.

The beauty in the colours – how the greens changed from lime to moss, forest to verdant, the call of the cuckoo, and learning to determine yarrow from hemlock. It was an awakening for me to feel like I was remembering the wisdom of the woods and rediscovering my love of nature; native plants as well as the beauty of what it meant to Mother together. The energy of 'Mother' vibrating all around in a space quiet and still.

During this time, I became more connected to my body, my breath and I stepped back onto my yoga mat (which had taken me 10 months).

Whilst pregnant again, I felt called to train as a yoga teacher and I relished doing something solely for me. It was the medicine I needed. A chance to meet me and reconnect with myself.

Ten moons pregnant (40 weeks + 10 days) and we had to move again. So, on a hot summer's evening on the day I signed papers to buy our house, I gave birth to my second son in the pool at home surrounded by boxes with just my breath to guide me. It was yet another indescribably amazing experience. The touching of his head under the water will remain with me forever, as I surrendered into the happening of childbirth. Another awakening, another homecoming, another otherworldly sensation. In Mexican culture, it is believed women travel to the stars to collect the souls of their baby and then return to Earth. It felt exactly like that returning from an ethereal space.

A week later, we moved house and six months later, lockdown arrived.

One night in April, my business baby, 'Glow' was born. It was a calling to support women at this unprecedented time. The pregnant women and the new Mothers left to fend for themselves at a time when community and family were needed the most. Women birthing on their own, met with masked faces or unable to have the homebirths they so desperately desired.

I felt my Grandmother guiding me in a way that is hard to explain. Her work as a midwife bubbling up within me. And so it was to be, that working in the magical birth space came to fruition. I specialised in pre and postnatal yoga and worked holistically, delving deep into the realms of spiritual birth keeping and Mothering. Using lockdown as a soul retreat – signing up for group courses and women's wellness masterclasses. Soaking up as much wisdom as I could.

That spring, a dream seed was planted, and I discovered my soul purpose; to ensure women were held in a safe space at this sacred time of creation. To walk with them on this path, positively sharing tools and resources to enable them to bring new life Earth-side. To birth like a Goddess and to Mother that way too.

There are no experts in Mothering, for the nuances and complexities are much too great... but I can be an expert in my own Mother Energy, and that is something we can all embrace. To let the perception of what others think disappear and to take ownership of our choices and decisions, as well as knowing what being a Mother means to us.

What I have learned, these past years, is that womanhood is all about the collective, a sisterhood and community of women. Women standing in their sovereignty, with or without children, with or without careers, with or without men. It is a forcefield of the most mystical energy that is lighting us all up and carrying us towards our truth.

On the day of my birth – the becoming a Mother – I arrived home to my truest essence. A door to another realm opened and a powerful container for the Divine Feminine, the Goddess and the Creatrix right at the centre, showed itself to me.

My Motherhood is being a stay-at-home mum and wellness entrepreneur. A woman who has created a life that fits within my own vision for living. A woman who enjoys making a home, because I never truly felt I had this soul space growing up. It is to try my best to be present, to seek out new ways of Mothering and to always ask for help.

It is to witness other Mothers, without judgement, and to acknowledge the differences between one another. Learning this craft by making mistakes and getting it wrong, but then consciously doing it differently next time.

My Motherhood involves Mothering together, in the woodland, the parks, at play dates or the school gates, along with other Mothers who are Mothering their way and managing their own queendom without apology or shame.

Remembering that Motherhood is hard and full of complex nuances. It is to recall we were never supposed to Mother alone and that we are all raising the next generation as one. We are healing wounds and caressing scars along this path, as we grow as individuals and as women. It takes a mighty village, and it takes time. Time to find your people, your village and time to trust them too.

I feel honoured to be a Mother, to have unlocked and discovered this enchanted realm. From feeling vulnerable and untethered, to eventually embracing the love and wisdom of others to help guide me forward and ground me. I have met wonderful women, joined circles and expanded my learning, becoming more in tune; with my environment and really trusting in what I know to be *my* wisdom, *my* intuition and *my* instinctual Mother Energy.

My Motherhood has been (and still is) a winding track of acceptance, hormones, love and loss. Women are shapeshifters in body, heart and mind, and to me this is the beauty of it all. We are always changing, our bodies confirm this each month with our moon bleed, and we are reminded yet again of our power to grieve, to heal, to bud, to bloom, to glow in our power, and then to retreat. Like the wildflowers, we are a part of this movement of nature, this natural cyclical motion that is ever revolving.

Our own golden thread on the loom of life is not always visible to other people, but it can be felt deeply within our being. You might call it a feeling, or you may know the whisper as your intuition, or perhaps you refer to this magnetic charge as your spirit. But whatever it is to you, and whatever meaning it may hold, I hope you know it circumnavigates our world, pulsing through the cosmos and connects us all.

This is the power of the Mother; The Great Mother who unites our community to the earth and the sky. She resides at the very centre of each of us.

My gift to you is COURAGE...

COURAGE to realise you won't know everything at first, but you will be learning so much, and it does get easier. You are doing brilliantly.

COURAGE to ask for help when you need it. You will need it. Please reach out and seek the support! There is no shame in this, and we learn from others.

COURAGE to make mistakes, and then to be kind to yourself when you make them. We all make mistakes and wish we could have done things a little differently, but be kind to yourself. Without making mistakes we can't see another way, so try to embrace these teachings. They are there to guide you. There is a lot of adjusting to do.

COURAGE to accept that no day will be the same. Some days will be tough and other days will be dreamy. It's all part of the ebb and flow and natures rebalancing. Roll with the waves and remember each day will pass, and every morning a new dawn will rise.

COURAGE to appreciate that babies/children/other people have their own agenda. You can only control your own responses and actions. You won't always be able to figure out a quick fix, so breathe and do your best.

COURAGE to trust yourself and your body. You know you. Have confidence in Mother Nature, she knows her s***. Tune in and listen deeply. Head outside, breathe in the wind and feel her on your skin. You know what's best for you, your family and your kingdom.

COURAGE to believe whatever you are feeling (happy, sad, lonely, overwhelmed, discouraged, scared, excited, overjoyed, delighted, fretful, anxious, calm) will pass and it will be OK. It can be frightening but embrace it. You are amazing and sometimes there are no words to express how we feel. That's the magic. Some things are meant to be felt, not seen.

COURAGE to step outside into the big wide world with pride and prowess. Be your inner lioness and don't worry what other people think.

COURAGE to rest and take time for yourself. We are all healing from something, and we need time to rest. The Mother Energy is strong and potent, powerful and intense at times. So honour this and know that stopping is not a sign of weakness, but a sign of strength, as you acknowledge your rhythms.

COURAGE to simply be. This is the Creatrix within you. To call in the guides and Goddesses, to show you another way and explore new routes and options.

COURAGE to talk to other mums and be open. Listen to their experiences and share your own. It takes a mighty good village to hold such wonder women. Have the COURAGE to listen to yourself over anyone else and COURAGE to do it your way. Be wild and to use Glennon Doyle's phrase ... "be untamed. You do you, and I'll do me."

COURAGE to step out of the room and take a couple of deep breaths. The French call it 'Le pause' – a moment or two before reacting, allowing time to access a situation. This is my top tip!

COURAGE to love yourself. You are the most important being, so self-care is paramount.

COURAGE to know that you are enough. "You got this Mama!"

You are Queen of your own Kingdom!

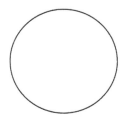

RAGE AGAINST THE MACHINE

By Emma While

I am a strong, confident, capable, stubborn woman.

I love a good argument and never hold back from telling it exactly like it is.

And yet throughout my pregnancy and Motherhood, I have been infantilised, ignored, demeaned, patronised, overlooked and undermined. From my birthing preferences to my concerns over my son's reflux, continual crying, shitty sleep and discomfort, all the way through to his schooling and pretty much everything in between.

There's a special look people get on their face when they find themselves in the presence of an inconvenient Mother, and it's not a good one.

Specifically, the things I've noticed people like to dismiss (especially if they go against what I 'should' be doing, which, quite frankly, they usually do), are my judgements, my body, my intuition, my boundaries, my dignity, my concerns, my opinions and my wishes...

So not much then.

And usually the people doing the dismissing are people in 'authority,' 'experts' of some description to whom I am expected to give away my power, simply because they've earned this 'expert' status from some official body somewhere.

It used to happen so frequently during my early Motherhood (my son is now 6) that I just got used to it. But I wasn't expecting it to happen again quite so recently.

A few months ago I discovered a lump in my breast and was referred to the specialist screening clinic.

I was absolutely terrified. And alone, thanks to Covid restrictions.

In the middle of poking officiously around in my boobs, the (female) doctor raised the option of having a scan as well as the physical exam, just to be sure. This also led her to ask if I was breastfeeding. To which I replied without thinking, 'Yes.' She asked how long I have been nursing for? And I said, "Five years."

At which point the tone of the meeting shifted entirely.

Bearing in mind that I was there to ascertain the health of my own breasts and in fact my own life, as a woman, a person, a self and not a Mother, and not there to discuss my son or our nursing relationship whatsoever, what happened next totally floored me.

Because the doctor carrying out my breast screening check took it upon herself to lecture me about how I should no longer be breastfeeding my (five year old) son. She spoke to me, at length, like a small child, spouted what I know to be a whole load of nonsense with no scientific basis whatsoever, scolded me for my ridiculousness and told me in no uncertain terms to stop.

It wasn't even anything to do with my health or the health of my breasts she was 'advising' me on at this point, she was lecturing me about the problems it would cause my son and how it would cause him to become too attached.

I mean... no words. I'm sure I'm not the only pregnant/new Mother who received the lecture about how breastfeeding lowers your chances of breast cancer so you should definitely do it. Apparently this breast cancer lady hadn't had that memo.

Now, when my son was younger I expected this 'discussion' to come up every time we met with a health visitor or such like and so was always prepared for it (and secretly looking forward to it to be honest) and gave as good as I got. But on this occasion I was taken entirely unawares and was just too shocked to have a comeback. In fact, I was utterly speechless, which for anybody who knows me is an incredibly rare occurrence.

So I smiled meekly, hastily scrabbled to get my clothes back on, nodded and off I trotted, head hung in shame like the naughty little girl I had been.

I must note at this point that she didn't find a lump, but the relief I should have felt at that news had been totally overshadowed by the bollocking I'd been given and my subsequent shame response.

As I walked back to the car, wondering what on earth had just happened, the small, scared, silly little girl mode I had retreated into in the face of her attack gradually subsided and was replaced by an absolute infernal rage. I. was. So. angry.

BOILING with fury.

Because what she had just done had been SO inappropriate on so many levels. SO many levels.

1. It was absolutely not her place and totally out of her remit to comment on my nursing relationship with my son. Yes it is her place to give me factual information about the ability to scan or not, or the efficacy of scanning or not whilst breastfeeding, but that is where her input on the matter should have both started and ended.

2. What she gave me was her moral judgement and opinion, presented as fact. As far as I'm aware, whilst her work centres around breasts, she is neither an expert, nor has expert experience of either the physiology or the emotional aspects of using those breasts in a nursing relationship.

3. Much of what she said I knew already, or now know having fact checked her afterwards, to be scientifically incorrect. Including the bit about not being able to do the scan if I was breastfeeding 'still.'

4. And not only that, she said it all without permission, without warning and without knowing anything about me, my son or our journey.

5. She gave it in a tone that was incredibly aggressive, accusatory and rude.

6. AND this (one way) conversation happened in the middle of an incredibly sensitive, vulnerable moment for me emotionally AND physically, not to mention the fact I was lying down with my tits out while she stood over me in a power suit.

She crossed a line. She steamrollered over a boundary. It was a total violation on various levels.

Not only all of that but the letter she then wrote to my GP afterwards was totally patronising and dismissive, included information I had not only not shared with her but that was totally irrelevant to the issue in hand, and essentially made me out to be a neurotic weirdo.

Which I may very well be. But that is my choice and neither here nor there when it comes to whether or not I have a breast lump. Her personal opinion of whether or not I 'should' be breastfeeding should never, ever have been presented in that way, at that moment, by that person. Or in fact ever.

To clarify at this point...I am more than fully aware that nursing a giant 5 (now 6) year old seems weird to very many people. I am fully aware that many of those people would go so far as to say it's disgusting. And they're allowed to have their opinion. And they absolutely must not, under any circumstances abuse their position of (perceived) power to push those opinions onto other people.

And there are two reasons I put that 'perceived' in there.

The first is that we have been taught from a very early age that there are certain types of people we respect, look up to, fear even. Doctors, teachers, politicians, policemen...people who have been given positions of authority in society, who know more than us about specific areas, who have the ability to help or punish us depending on the circumstances.

Because of this social conditioning, we've somehow decided that they DO know better than us about almost anything. We have afforded them more power than really either their experience, expertise or standing affords them. Because this lady was a doctor I was supposed to accept her forthright opinion as fact and go do something about it.

But really she's just some woman who decided to become a boob doctor.

She knows far LESS than me about MY breastfeeding relationship with my son. She DOES know more about breast cancer and how to spot and treat it...but she veered outside of that remit and still spoke with the same amount of authority about something else (that I hadn't even asked her to).

AND I let her. And that's the second reason that perception is key.

In that moment, I perceived her to be the expert, to know more than me, to have a greater say in those things than I did. Her words only had power over me because I let them. Because in that moment, vulnerable, terrified and lying half naked on a couch, my shell was off and those words got right to the squishy bit in the middle. I had let my guard down, I wasn't ready for battle. NOR was I feeling centred, grounded or strong.

Had I been a) dressed and b) feeling more 'myself,' I would have put my hand up and said, "I'm going to stop you there. Thank you for the information re the scan. I will do my own research and consider what you've said, but right now my breastfeeding relationship with my son is absolutely not up for discussion."

Words I have uttered many times before.

And the thing that makes me really angry, is if those kinds of situations can make a bolshy, obstinate, argumentative gobshite like ME a quivering wreck, what the bloody fuck is it doing to everybody else!?

THAT is what really makes my blood boil. Knowing that other less confident, more sensitive, vulnerable and marginalised women are being manipulated, dismissed, demeaned, ignored, lied to and patronised like this every single day.

And not just by doctors who should know better. But by their own partners, their Mothers, the woman in the shop queue, the media and life at large.

How many women give up their dream of a homebirth because they were told they 'had to' birth in the hospital?

How many women stop exclusively breastfeeding because they're told they 'have to' supplement?

How many Mothers leave their babies to cry because they've been told it's the only way?

How many pregnant women subject themselves to a diabetes glucose test because they're told they 'have to'?

How many women don't homeschool their children because they're told they 'have to' send them to school?

There are so many things we are told we 'have to' do. When we don't.

Because not everybody knows they're allowed to ask questions. To argue. To demand more information. To refuse to comply. To seek alternatives. To challenge.

Not everybody knows they're allowed to disagree. To say No.

Not everybody knows that other people's opinions aren't fact and that we don't have to accept them as OUR own truth.

Not everybody knows we don't have to do what other people think we should do, or want us to do.

Or that it's OK if people don't like it when we don't.

Not everybody knows that actually, this isn't 'just how it is,' and that we really do get to choose how WE want to do it.

And even when they 'know', they have no idea how. Because nobody else ever showed them. And it's terrifying as fuck to go against everything we've ever known.

I have spent so much of my life making myself wrong.

The encounter with the lady in the breast cancer clinic was no exception. I allowed it to make me wrong. To make my choices wrong. To make my relationship with my son wrong.

She made me feel like it wasn't OK.

And she was right. It isn't OK.

It isn't OK that Mothers everywhere are being made to feel like that every. Single. Day.

That wrongness I sensed, wasn't about me. It was about her. And everything she represents.

And every day I vow, even more strongly, to never let myself take that on as my own again and to shout it from the rooftops for other Mothers everywhere to hear it as their permission slip to do the same.

WAKE UP MAMA

By Dulcie Batt

I am Mama of four, without a Mama, and my children have never had a Grandma. I was just pregnant with my firstborn, when my lovely Mama died. This wake-up call had a profound impact on me and my approach to Mamahood.

Triggering a deep dive, to question everything.

Following my soul's call to normalise and honour Mama's intense feelings on their journey, inspiring them to activate their Joy and uplift their experience. If you want to consciously navigate your Mamahood path feeling fulfilled, aware and lit up by life, this is for you.

I believe with all my heart that we are joyful beings, that Joy is at our centre, as our birthright. We come into the world as bundles of Joy, expressed so freely as children and hidden under layers of responsibility as we grow. As Mamas, we are aware of the unspoken cultural law that it is selfish to focus on our joy ahead of our children's needs – but my darling, what is your dearest wish? For your kids to be healthy and Joyful. It is your radical responsibility to MODEL that to your children. How will they know what joyful looks like if they haven't seen it?

Joy is integral to you. Her light will never extinguish in your lifetime and when you pass, she will continue to shine in those who are your legacy. When you nourish, nurture and honour her she radiates brightly. She is the spark in your eye, the cheeky twinkle, the glow that you emanate. A wellspring of goodness to serve you and essential FUEL in Mamahood.

Imagine having a Joy tank inside you that fuels life and authentic living as a full representation of yourself. With such energetic power, bringing boldness, passion, warmth to your bones, so you shine and light the path for others. Unlike happiness, joy pervades regardless of external factors – she is profoundly deep and the true contentment at the very heart of you.

Have you ever thought about your connection to your Joy in this way?

I believe we choose our parents, and my soul chose mine with intent – they are exactly who I need, to evolve and fulfil my life's purpose. My childhood was Joyful and my lovely Mama had the very opposite experience as a child. I am so grateful that she chose to raise me, with all the love she never had. My dear Dad lost his Mama, my namesake Dulcie, to cancer when he was just 25 – she is my original guardian angel.

I always knew I would have four children. What I didn't know is that grief would almost overcome the start of my journey. Simultaneously holding the news of my first pregnancy and death of my Mama, was utterly confusing – pure delight and complete heartbreak. I desperately wanted to drown and numb my sorrows, but new life had chosen me and the due date was 08.12.04 – exactly nine months after my Mama died.

In the circle of life, dear Rex chose his own birthday and 13 months later, I birthed darling Ruby. During this intense initial period as a Mama, the invaluable wisdom that I sought was from the one person who was no longer able to gift it to me. The lack of her love Earthside, left an enormous hole in my life.

With two young babies in tow and much unprocessed grief, my coping mechanism became the art of numbing and switching off. I threw myself 100% into caring for my babies and disregarded me, until I felt like a stranger in the mirror. I lost confidence in my working self, could hardly imagine me as the thriving city worker I used to be. I might have looked as though I had it together, but felt as if I was simply going through the motions. You know when you feel once removed, viewing yourself from above as if your life is happening to someone you're watching in a movie?

Looking back, I wish I had stayed in touch with what lit me up. For me and my family. At the time, I felt as though allowing myself to be joyful was dishonouring my Mama's memory – how could I be Joyful without her? My babies often delighted me but outside of them I didn't feed my Joys. I retreated, the colour slowly seeped from life and I became used to numb, grey living where nothing could really hurt me, but increasingly nothing could lift me either. This was mid-lane malaise living, we moved to Surrey, my babes were happy and I felt trapped. My husband sensing my discomfort, said one morning that he'd have the kids and I could go and do whatever I wanted.... I literally had no idea what to do...

The Universe worked her strange magic, as is often the way when life needs to be shaken up. There were a range of health issues in our little family, heart murmurs, suspected meningitis, prolonged hospital stays. Then total burn out, agonising fractured vision headaches and brain scans for my gorgeous husband. All the signs were to WAKE up to life and what she is really about. To tune into our hearts, articulate our desires and follow them boldly – they were Joy, Presence and Freedom.

Within weeks we had sold much of what we owned, including our house, taken a health-enforced sabbatical from work and bought a boat. We picked her up in Croatia and found ourselves with our bags on the quay, standing next to our new home. This was the space we needed to reconnect and live our lives to the beat of our own drum, rather than what our society dictates. With four and three year old Rex and Ruby, we set sail and continued our travels around the world for the next year, escaping from life and her excessive demands as we knew them.

It was a truly EPIC year where I allowed myself to start feeling again, really feeling, the full expanse of life. Everything felt brighter. I felt more in touch with my true self, not the damped down, responsible and grieving Mama version of me that had become my new normality.

One pivotal evening with the babes asleep in their bunks, I was meditating on the bow, the sun on my face, the breeze in my hair, listening to the soothing sound of the waves against the boat and some magic happened in my heart. I gazed at the vast vista, mesmerised by the sunlight twinkling on the waves – the sparkling light feeling like the closest thing to heaven. I tuned in to my Mama's spirit and her energy washed through my body like a wave of the deepest love. Tears streamed from my eyes and the message came through, loud and clear. As is the deep wish of every Mama, she wanted me to live Joyfully. Honouring her spirit with deep connection to my JOY. Opening my heart to allow the full experience of all of life. Keeping her spirit alive by allowing her to flow through me and continually return to my Joy. Back to Joy, back to Love. Back to Joy, back to Love. Through all of life's twists and turns, this would be my path. I knew that my destiny was to live this new existence, complete my family and hold space for women who are going through the transition of Mamahood. I will never forget that evening, it was my wake-up call. I cried for days afterwards, cleansing tears, the grief washing away and my Joyful birthright energy at my centre rekindled, reawakened and activated.

We returned to the UK, pregnant with my third and settled by the sea in Poole. Baby Jago arrived, bringing his own unique magic and total inspiration for baby four. After three medicalised births, I heard whispers of women having empowered births – transcendent experiences where they felt like a Goddess Warrior, totally in touch with their own power. Knowing baby four would be my last I sought out how to achieve this wonder experience myself and discovered the power of hypnobirthing. My fourth labour was drug free, without medical assistance and deep trust in my innate body wisdom. I felt so incredibly in my power. As I birthed our Liberty into my arms, I said to my husband, "I have to share this wisdom with other Mamas."

Fast forward to now, nine years on – I am a Mama guide, hosting retreats with Midwives, holding space for classes and events created to connect Mamas to their Joy. Using my training in pregnancy and postnatal yoga, hypnobirthing, Qoya and NLP – all practices devoted to women remembering who they are at their centre, coming together in community and feeling good in Mamahood. Doing soul purpose work that I love, with my Mama as my angel co-worker.

There is so much that I want to share with you and Mama let's start with pregnancy and birth – the sacred rite of passage and time when many women look inside deeper than they ever have before. You're aware of new sensations as your body changes and is no longer 'somebody' you know. Tuning into your body's whispers, you pull away from the busyness of the outside world. This call inwards is such a special and essential time to really get to know yourself. What makes you tick, what you truly desire, what makes you feel truly alive? Create your Joy List and discover your 'Joydentity' before you birth your baby Earthside.

So many of us know what we don't want in life, but are less articulate with our desires. How do you wish to live your life? What kind of Mama do you want to be? Which past family patterns, emotional legacies do you want to share with your child, which do you wish to avoid? What does your heart say?

May you be curious and view becoming a Mama as the start of a lifetime of adventure. May I share my key Mamahood insights, born from curiosity in mine and my clients' experience. Woven with lessons from my Mama's spirit, that I'll pass onto my children and to you through the gift of this book. Five simple lessons that allow deeper connection to your JOY so you can rely on it in your life as a lasting state of being. Aptly the first letters of each of the five words spell CUPPA – so grab yourself one and indulge:

1. **Consciousness** – Matrescence, the art of becoming a Mama, is a rite of passage bringing great opportunity to raise our consciousness. Our identity shifts, we are not who we used to be. We imagine we

might go back, epitomised by the obsession of so many to get 'back into their jeans' post baby. Mama, there is no going back, instead a metamorphosis, moving forward, an ever evolving being. Our children are our spiritual teachers, testing and uplifting us more than anyone. May we be humbled by our learnings. Note how we are triggered, look deeply as to why that might be. Use the power of the pause, to give ourselves chance to respond, rather than react. Build curiosity around our boundaries and response. Be kind in our words and actions and apologise when we are not.

This is a time to consciously connect with our Mama tribe – our community who lift and support us. Consciously be aware of how we speak to ourselves and our children. Consciously articulate our desires, know and honour what lights us up as we evolve. Know that true connection with our children, as we raise them as conscious beings, begins with connection with ourselves.

2. **Unconditional Love** – How would it feel if you chose pregnancy as the time to begin an unconditional love affair with yourself? Honouring the gift of Mama Nurture – feeling the feels that bring you down and loving yourself anyway. Loving yourself enough through the highs that you SOAK them in, allowing them to boost you. Committing to this self-nourishment as though you are someone very special, because you ARE.

The good girl conditioning that so many of us were raised with, tells us that there is nothing worse than a Mama who doesn't feel like spending every single minute with her little angels and yet the truth is, we don't – and the guilt layers up. We turn inward with self-criticism and this habit of self-attack is so common that it's invisible to most of us.

Note the voices in your head, the mind chatter your internal 'shitty committee.' Recognise that you are not 'them', you are the 'observer' of them. Consciously move from criticism and note all your big and little wins instead – identify yourself as a Mama who is doing her best, which is more than enough. It is deeply healing to honour self-celebration. Love yourself unconditionally, as fiercely as you do your child. Lead the way in this act of Joyful rebellion and light the path for others!

3. Presence – is one of the most essential and challenging qualities in Mamahood. Don't you agree that our human tendency is to spend most of our time locked in our heads, rather than the current experience of life as she unfolds? Fretting about the past, prophesising, lamenting, feeling guilty... Yet, what do we each truly DESIRE? To feel good. To feel in touch with our Joy and She lives in the present. We can remember past and imagine future Joys, but we can only experience her right NOW.

Our children demand our presence through the emotional rollercoaster of Mamahood. Presence over a broader emotional spectrum, from deep despair to sheer delight. There is often resistance to this, as we push away the negative feelings, the exhaustion, the stress, the guilt, the rage. If we resist rather than feel, numb the lows, we narrow our living range and feel numb to the highs too. My experience of this was magnified by grief. With our life experience limited to 'comfortable,' our Joy is rarely activated. Is this real living? Noooo! And our children model us – so by squashing down our uncomfortable feelings and limiting our capacity for Joy, we teach them to do the same. Instead, choose to be awake, feel and embrace it all. Know that emotions are 'energy in motion' – they pass, deepen our resilience and enrich our lives.

As the youngest of four, my lovely Liberty insists on my presence, by taking hold of my face with both her hands and turning it to face her, whenever she wants my full attention. She's a constant reminder to deep dive into present moment living. In our rush culture, we adopt the 'in a minute' mindset – I'll watch your dance/look at your picture in a minute – once the washing up/cooking/work is done. Though sometimes unavoidable, it's often habitual, and in denying ourselves these moments in the progress of an often banal task, we deny ourselves the Joy of connection.

Being present to Joy can feel vulnerable – because if you admit to it, it can be taken away. Recently, I kissed Jago goodnight and he declared, "I LOVE loving you Mama"... oh my heart, a moment so saturated in deliciousness, almost too much to bear. It is so easy to brush these moments away, rush them, but Mama please plug in and PAUSE a while. Deliciously indulge and top up your Joy tank, breathe in and marinade. THIS is where the magic lies. This is fuel for the next chapter on the rollercoaster of life – so if you plummet downwards after this moment, you have fuel in the engine, you can survive, even thrive in what life throws at you because you KNOW you are part of something so good. So primal. So essential.

4. Positive Perspective – We hold such incredible power in the focus of our attention, and energy grows where attention goes. Being a Mama has such a weight of responsibility. There is so much that could go wrong, but there is so much that could go right. When stuck in a negative perspective, I love Tara Brach's RAIN approach – 'Recognise, Allow, and Investigate' the feeling and 'Nurture' yourself through it. I always increase it to RAINBOW because this technique always 'Boosts Our Wellbeing'!

There is a real sense as a Mama that acknowledging Joy is tempting fate and will somehow bring about something negative. I spent much of my early Mamahood with this perspective, worrying through the good times, waiting for the next catastrophe to happen. Young kids tend to enter several calamities each day but when you are bracing yourself for them, you are actually drawing that experience into your reality. Instead, focus on the good, the positives and the law of attraction will work in your favour.

Mindset matters – in pregnancy, labour, birth and beyond. Even in times of great distress, there is a gift, a lesson and a reframe. Perspective myopia rules all too often and a broader perspective is gold. That feeling we get when we are at the airport or awed by nature. This recognition of being part of something so much greater than our immediate reality, minimises our problems and deepens our sense of connection to others.

No matter what is unfolding, there is always HOPE. Feel it all and Harness Only Positive Emotions. Be aware of how perspective can seep or deepen your joy.

5. Acceptance – We enter Mamahood with expectations and the Joy hurdle is the adjustment of our expectations vs the reality. We want our kids to be confident and this requires our curiosity around knowing our child, discovering and supporting who we find them to be, rather than who we expect them to be.

Acceptance over resistance, fuels Joy.

Mamahood brings an opportunity to learn and adopt our child's pace. Often this requires us to accept the call to slow down and savour living in a whole new way. As a fast-moving creature, who deemed 'doing' as productive, I had such resistance to slowing down. Through burnout, I have realised the hard way that 'Being' is super productive and essential modelling to our kids. More than ever, Mamahood is a time to Invest in Rest!

If you can't bear a particular situation and wish for a 'beam me up Scotty' moment, then use it as a Joy Rocket for what you desire. Moving from "I don't want to be stuck in this house with this screaming baby" to "I want to get out and have some fun!" creates coping space with what's unfolding and gets added to your Joy List as a desire to be honoured soon. Adopting the wise Buddhist philosophy 'this too will pass' is useful too – it is all a phase, be present through it, it will pass. As needy as your baby may be, this relentless phase of teething, not sleeping, will pass, as will your days of holding them in your arms. Treasure the moments – there is always Joy if you look for it.

There will be such positivity and negativity. You will feel Mama guilt for not living up to your expectations, and Mama rage for life not living up to your expectations. Leave those expectations at the door, accept what is right now and create desires for how you wish to shape your future. Expectations are often fuelled by comparison to others and comparison is the thief of Joy.

No amount of your worry or guilt can change the past or future, and will always reduce your enjoyment of the present. As Eckhart Tolle says, "Accept – then act. Whatever the present moment contains, accept it as if you had chosen it. Always work with it, not against it...This will miraculously transform your whole life."

To sum up...

Being a Mama is incredibly challenging: often yearned for, meaningful, paramount, full of love, Joy and exhaustion, resistance, fear and fury. Where we love most, we hurt most and it can feel like a battle, but let's reframe it as a dance – between wanting to spend time with your children and needing space. A dance to the beat of your own drum. You get to write your own story, there is no perfect narrative to fit. You do you, Mama.

Mamahood requires constant calibration, teaching, listening and modelling behaviour. And Mama, you are likely to be your best self when you know and trust yourself with all your wonderful strengths and vulnerabilities.

May you accept this as the deepest journey of love that you will ever take... love for your child and yourself.

Taking Radical Responsibility for your mind, body, birth, baby, and how you feel as a Mama.

Honour your daily CUPPA and fuelling your Joy tank.

Know what lights you up and prioritise space for that every day, even if some days it is just for a moment. You are a beautiful, Joyful, conscious being – create space for her and connect into THAT self with love, understanding and positivity.

You have an extraordinary life force within you. May you nurture your Joy and experience the full colour spectrum of Mamahood, in all her technicolour glory.

Say goodbye to grey living and welcome to the Joyful Rebellion for Mamas. It will serve you and your children well. May you forever be tapped into the pulse of life and feeling truly alive!

LIFE CHANGES MOTHER

By Alison Gregory Cooper

Sixteen years ago, my life was very different. I was living in London, working a corporate job and living the life of my dreams with my then husband – until the day came that I gave up my job to become a Mum. Little did I know how much this was going to change me or my entire life!

The birth of my first son was long and traumatic and he had to be taken away from me for some emergency care. So, after having gone through a full twenty-four-hour labour and feeling exhausted, upset, and angry that the birth hadn't gone to plan, I fell asleep. But, when I woke up, I wasn't the same person. I had feelings that were less desirable and not of my previous fun, excited and happy self. Though this was the catalyst to my Spiritual Awakening, I had always had an interest in tarot and the paranormal and was a quiet, sensitive child. I'm not one for holding on to old stories, so I only include general statements of my experiences as some of you may resonate with them.

Possibly like many of you, I experienced a lot of traumas and dark nights of the soul, including what a doctor may call depression or even delusion. But it wasn't until much later, I realised it was all just bringing me back to myself. Many of the incidents I went through enabled me to feel the presence of God/Source, Angels and other beings that cannot be seen with our eyes. This is now happening for more and more people faster than ever. I have absolute trust and belief in these things because of my personal experiences, but it is not for me to project these on to anyone. I simply share, for it may help someone going through similar experiences. Many of us are here at this time to step into our own Divinity in order to create heaven on Earth. Starseeds, lightworkers, wayshowers and healers are HuMan conduits, bringing light and codes to Earth to assist in the ascension process at this time.

For thousands of years, women have been taken advantage, of as men have been unable to see, or care what they were doing to them. Shaming and abusing the feminine, not listening, making them feel less worthy. Yet the feminine aspect is within both male and female bodies, however you may identify.

So *Wake up Mother*, for me, cannot be just about women because the feminine and masculine principles are within ALL.

For years I was all over the place reacting often from the wounded masculine and feminine principles within me. I had learnt in childhood not to trust men or women, so I had a lot of walls built around me. Many of our ancestors were deeply traumatised, abused, raped, and forced into marriages that they wouldn't have chosen.

Let's not forget the witches who were in tune with their intuition and healed with nature, but were silenced, burnt, or hung and made to look evil. The women who experienced the unthinkable, I deeply honour them all.

Most of us have all had past lives in male and female bodies. Many of you reading this are likely here to heal these wounds at this time, so that you do not have to continue to suffer. And you do not continue to carry them through lifetime to lifetime or through bloodlines.

Whether you are aware or not, we are moving into a new way of being, a new age. This is no different from any previous 'age' in history such as the Ice Age or Stone Age, for example. The only difference is that *we* are living and experiencing this change here and *now*.

A New Earth cannot be created using the old ways and it isn't yet fully apparent what this will look like for anyone, as it is being created moment to moment in the collective consciousness.

I deeply honour our ancestors. They are within you and I, but now they stand by our sides asking us not to go back to these ways. To stop reliving the stories, to heal them, to forgive and accept the learning in order to create better.

Yes, let's be inspired by aspects of community and sharing. But to create a better world there needs to be more harmony and balance within each of *us* first. It is only with this harmony and balance within each of us that we can create a world of peace and love, not out of fear and trauma, anger, or rage.

I deeply honour the wounded men too. And however you identify, I fully respect and honour that. I am talking here about a female body and a male body and the feminine and masculine principles within ALL of humanity for we ALL carry both aspects within. Men have had to deny their intuition and feminine principles as well, encouraged to fight and 'be a man.' Many were taught that it was OK to take advantage of women, to silence them, to sexualise them, that men were more powerful and had to be listened to.

This has taken its toll as well. It's not just about the body you are in, as men have also found themselves in relationships where the woman was leading from their wounded masculine principle and abused the man who was leading with his wounded feminine principle. I deeply honour all the men who have also struggled and were conditioned into these ways of being and I honour everyONE who has done and is doing healing within themselves and everyONE on Earth at this time living through this time of transformation.

I do feel that there's a fine line with the rising of the Divine Feminine as I see many Women's Circles and now also Men's gatherings appearing. Indeed, this has been necessary for the uprising of humanity, but I also wonder if this still perpetuates separation in society and so personally every space I hold I welcome ALL into.

As the world was forced to slow down over the last few years, it was perfectly orchestrated for more people to experience an awakening as humanity had no choice but to stop and spend more time at home. In doing this, each began to see and feel what's important in their life and where they had been lied to.

They began to connect more with themselves as they reconnected with nature, feeling the calm unconditional love of Gaia. With this open heart, many suddenly feel what love really is and it is not what we were taught love is.

When you feel the sun on your face, you may feel soothed and loved because you are not separate from the Father, The Universe, Source, God, Allah, or whatever name you may personally use.

The deeper you go with your shadow and the unravelling of the traumas you carry, the old ways of living no longer feel good to you, the more you see through the conditioning that has happened in your childhood and all around you.

Of course, each person's experiences will be unique to feel less wanted emotions.

Many will not to look at their wounding, often because they are not aware of it and this should be respected with no judgement. This is what their soul has chosen and how we come into Unity Consciousness.

We were taught to call emotions 'negative' but these are in fact gifts. Every feeling and emotion is there to show you what *you* carry within *you* and not everyone likes to hear that. Indeed, some may say that this open's you up to feeling a lot of guilt, shame and blame towards yourself. Instead reacting and blaming others for how you feel became the norm but, it is exactly this place where the healing is found, this is the gift, the pot of gold.

We always had and have a choice in how we react to things going on around us.

It is only as you begin shedding the I-dentities built up around you, that you remember you are not here to be slaves to systems that drain your soul, your very own lifeforce. We all chose our parents, friends, and lovers to gift us the perfect opportunities of growth and learning on Earth school, at this time of ascension. One by one, as each person continues to 'awaken,' as each ONE realises that no matter how many things you buy, how much money you have in the bank, or how big your house is, they don't satisfy your soul. As nice as those things are to have, you often end up in a perpetual cycle of wanting more and more.

Welcome to Earth school, it's a beautiful design!

Dear Children of the Light I come to you now as the Divine Mother.

You are not separate from me. I am no bigger than you and yet in your earthly bodies it seems so. But you are so much more than you realise. What seems real to you is only a small percentage of what and who you really are. Let me hold you in my womb, feel my embrace as you connect with me on the Earth and in the waters. Give to me your frustrations and pain. Let me hold you and nurture you. Speak to me in the field of dreams. I am always here for you

I am the Divine Mother and I love you unconditionally.

Sixteen years ago, if you had told me I would be a guide for others, channelling messages and healing, I would have laughed and called you crazy. But that's the thing about evolution, you don't know what's coming next and where it's taking you. Many have indeed called me crazy, but when you have this deep inner calling you can only push it away for so long. I didn't know for many years that I had already been channelling all my life, and I share this because I'm sure you have too, you just don't know what you don't know! Think back just five years ago and see how much you have changed, how much your own life has changed. When you become a Mother, it seems that you suddenly have this innate knowing. You know if your child is sick and you can pick out your baby's cry in a room full of many babies' crying. But this intuition has always been there waiting for you to acknowledge it. This is your Divine communication system; it is not seen, but felt.

Just a few years ago I never would have imagined channelling light language, let alone known what it was. But the more you heal, love, and surrender your ego mind, the more space you open yourself up to something new coming in.

Light Language is a Universal language that is spoken through the heart, bringing in healing codes, light and sacred geometry. You receive this data as a feeling or knowing as it bypasses the logical brain. And this is the point – to drop out of the ego conditioned mind and into our hearts. This is how we heal and create a better world where all can live in harmony. It is not to get rid of the ego but to bring the sacred heart and minds into union.

A OO Mi I Ko Na Ta I So Sha Na Na Ko Ma A Mu Ro Ta O Ma I Si Ko Na Na Tor I A Ka Na A Ki No I Li Sha-n OO Kor Maia Sa Na O Pah I Ka Si A Sha Na Mo Ya Ta Mor-a Ti I Na Ka Ya Qua Ti O Kor Sha

I am known within you as I am you.

I am of the Collective vibration knowing the Self as the Divine Mother within you.

I am the Spirit of your heart, a known power in the infinite creation of the collective

I am Spirit as Love in the Collective.

I am in the present moment, now, as the part of you that remains unified.

I am known now in the present, unified in the infinite Collective.

All that I share, is of course only my perspective from my own life experiences and everyONE of you will have your own, which should be honoured. I ask that you only take that which resonates and leave anything that doesn't. Which brings me on to Unity Consciousness. There has been a lot of talk about this recently in the spiritual community. Unity Consciousness does not mean that we are all the same or must agree with each other, because frankly, how boring would that be?! It means that we can all be fully in our own sovereignty, truth and knowing and allow others to have the same privilege through their own learning experiences and not judge them for it.

On this Earth school, you will always find that the right people enter your life at the right time to create experiences for you to learn from. Think about who's in your life now and ask yourself, what are they showing me about myself?

Let's look at the obvious one, our Mother. We all have a Mother, for we could not be here without one, however that looks for you. Have you ever said to yourself, 'I will never be like my Mum!'? None of us are born with preconceived ideas about either of our parents. It is only our experiences and traumas that shape our life through our thoughts and feelings which are built upon, as we go throughout our lives. So, I invite you to start with your own Mother and your relationship with her. Are you like her? Do you want to be? Why? I guarantee whatever your answers are that somewhere there are these qualities within you too and don't worry, this applies to anything that you deem to be 'good' as well as 'bad'. As a side note these words 'good and 'bad' are also a conditioning of the ego mind. It is only in letting go of these I-dentities that we build up around ourselves that we can return to our true self.

I believe becoming a Mother is the most life changing thing a woman can do. It's a whole new way of life and an ending of your old one, you will never NOT be a Mother again and nothing prepares you for that. Your previous I-dentities go out the window, at least for some time. But there are such precious gifts that can come from that too.

Children will highlight everything within you that's unhealed. And yet no matter what they do, you will love them anyway, even if you can't always show it, if this is what you learnt from your parents. Observe a child's innocence and their ability to just be themselves in each moment. Observe how you speak to them, because everything you say and do is shaping them in one way or another. This is where their I-dentity is built. The 'I' must do this, 'I'm only worthy, if I do this, 'I' mustn't do this, 'I' must be good, 'I' must let others go first, 'I' must be quiet, 'I'm not allowed to share how I feel, and all the other programs *you* might have been taught such as the famous 'money doesn't grow on trees' or 'if you eat all that now you won't have any left for tomorrow,' all scarcity programming.

If you can teach your children anything, teach them to love themselves, that they are always enough as they are without badges, certificates, grades, and achievements and that they are worthy of being heard, just as they are. Teach them to see and appreciate the abundance in nature and that which is around you. Teach your own inner child this and let go of the old programming.

All programs of the conditioned mind are simply learnt behaviours. It was never anyone's fault, not your mum, your dad, your auntie, uncle, brother or sister. We chose these people before we came to Earth school to learn from. The time is now to forgive any grievances, because the programs and I-dentities are not truth, but walls that are built up around you and others, as survival mechanisms.

EveryONE has their own lessons to learn and (if you have them), your children chose you to be their parent/guardian just as you have chosen them and indeed your own parents. So, know that ultimately you can never get it wrong, whatever experiences life brings, everyONE of them can be your teacher here on Earth school! EveryONE has a choice in how to live now, *today*. How we want to be in the world and relate with others is a choice though it often hasn't seemed that way.

What we heal for ourselves, we heal for all. To create new, we cannot keep reliving the past and keep telling the same old stories because this keeps the energy in the Collective – meaning you unknowingly keep creating the same situations in your life and in the world. Yes, we are here to honour it all, to feel it all, but it's also possible to forgive it all and to love it all, so that we can create better, from love and harmony, The New Earth.

You are not what happened to you – you are so much more.

You are worthy. You are loved. You are enough, just as you are now.

I invite you to say these affirmations to yourself daily and breathe each one in and out, watch how your life changes.

I am worthy

I love myself

I honour myself

I acknowledge myself

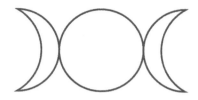

APOLOGIZING TO MY CHILDREN

By Carrie Myers

When my babies were born, I never dreamed I would go through some of the things I have now overcome. I never thought I would be apologizing to them for me checking out of life for more than a few years.

In 2014, I confirmed my husband was having an affair. Even though he ended it immediately, it had profound and lasting effects on me, mentally, emotionally, physically and spiritually. When such things floor us in our lives, we think we hide it, put a smile on our faces and no-one knows. But my kids knew. I shut down! I stopped cooking, stopped cleaning like I always have, stopped being available in most ways. I still took them to school, participated in all their activities, and took care of them the best I could, but I was not 'there.' I often would pack up and leave town, just to get away from my life. I ran away, but could not outrun my pain. I felt like I was no longer in my body, but watching a bad movie of what had become me. I looked into the mirror and did not even recognize the face staring back. I used alcohol to hide from myself, my husband and my heartache.

My husband and I started marriage counseling, but every time we left the counselors office, I felt like my heart was ripped from my chest and I was 'torn up' for what felt like days afterward. I never dreamed this would be my life, would be me.

I know my three amazing kids felt like I abandoned them, especially emotionally, during these years of me wallowing in my self-pity and heartaches. I clung to my pain so tightly, that I no longer recognized myself. My depression would send me back to bed many days, or out with a friend, who was also going through heartache, to drink and cry.

During these years, yes, years, of me wallowing, I journaled so much of my anger and hurt. One evening, as I walked in through the door, my middle child, met me right inside. He blatantly asked me, "Mom, who is Kelly?" I literally crumbled onto the stairs, as my heart fell out of my chest in the last pieces that remained.

I had a journal that I wrote the most details in, that I normally kept in my purse. At some point, I had left it on my nightstand. My daughter, my youngest, read it, then shared it with him. As he stood over me, as I sat in a puddle on the stairs, he asked me why I had not yet left his father. The look in my eyes told him. He said, "Because of us..." Yes, my children are a huge factor as to why I did not walk away from him in 2014.

And I would be lying if I said I was not somewhat relieved that my children finally knew the truth. My thought, "Maybe now they will understand why I am such a mess." As it turned out, this is the biggest factor that truly set me on my healing journey.

The next evening, we sat the kids down, over dinner, and told them the core of the truth. I was somewhat angry that they did not appear as hurt as I felt. They were not as upset with their father as I have been. However, I felt freedom in not trying to hide it anymore. I felt the freedom to be honest with my pain, myself and my kids. At the dinner table that cool fall evening, I stopped wallowing and started climbing out of my pit of despair.

I found a counselor for just me. I started taking intentional time for myself, without alcohol. I began writing instead of venting to my journal. My counselor led me toward talking to my children more about what had transpired and how it affected me over the years.

I demanded that my husband seek a counselor of his own, if he wanted me to stay in our marriage. I told him, I was not going to invest in healing myself and stay with him while he still sat in all the reasons – childhood trauma and self-doubt – that created our mess in the first place.

I was growing stronger. I began to truly heal and not live in the self-loathing pity that I had been swimming in for so very long.

Months went by, and I began to recognize glimmers of myself. Meditating and praying for guidance, for I knew I needed to talk to my children, apologize to them for my part in the chaos and numbness over the years. I rehearsed each word over and over in my mind. I cried as I thought about my confessions and truth throughout this journey. I beat myself up for harming my children, maybe even permanent damage, by checking out of life for so long. So many opportunities went by because I could not bring myself to say the words, I needed to say to each of them.

Then the time came. My husband was out of town and all three of the kids were home. They each needed their own conversation with me. I started out apologizing for allowing my emotional turmoil to overtake my love and dedication I have for each of them. Individually, I sat with them and cried. Each with their own love and tenderness, they listened. We cried, and I witnessed how differently they felt impacted by those years where I was spiritless and numb. As their mom, I let them down. I was not strong enough to deal with my pain and protect them from, well, me. I allowed my responsibility as mom to be buried by my brokenness and feelings of inadequacy. I took on all the burdens of my husband's affair as my fault. As if I were not good enough as a wife, I most certainly was not good enough as a Mother. I allowed his actions to determine who I was and was not.

Stripping away, what I thought was, my hiding places, allowed me to be honest with my kids and, ultimately, myself. That night, puddled on the stairs, confronted by my strong middle child, I thought, at the time, broke me into shards of irreparable pieces. However, it was the catalyst that began my healing, my excavation of my soul and a renewed outlook on who I truly am.

As a Mother, I thought I had failed them through my wallowing in the treacherous pits of heartache. As a Mother, I realized I did the best I could, at the time. As a Mother, I never once stopped loving or caring for my kids during this tumultuous time. As a Mother, I witnessed my children being compassionate, loving and forgiving. As a Mother, I am grateful that I had the strength to apologize to my kids for not only my selfishness during those years, but the way I truly shut them out, thinking I was protecting them. As a Mother, I have learned that honesty and transparency is always the best option when raising children. As a Mother, I am beyond grateful for their tender hearts and loving souls.

I know I will always have my regrets during my traumatic response to my husband's affair. But within that, I got the gift of witnessing the unconditional love my children have for me.

For this, I believe, is such a blessing.

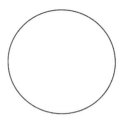

WHO IS MOTHER –
AND WHY IS SHE CRYING?

By Zoë Foster

There is a memory I carry with me as a daughter-turned-Mother. It serves as a reminder to me of the paradigm of Motherhood within our society – its many rigid expectations and fathoms of unsaid, suppressed traumas that Mothers bear through their lifetime.

I was 15, and quite possibly the most unsympathetic, emotionally blunt teen you could find. Everything irritated me, but especially my own Mum. I couldn't understand her on any level. I definitely didn't want to be her, and I rebelled against pretty much everything she was to me then. At the same time, I envied her: I felt like she had everything, and yet she never seemed happy.

One day, I found her sitting on the sofa very still, looking simultaneously occupied and vacant. "What's the matter?" I asked, not in a concerned tone but a charged mixture of surprise and scorn. To my utter disbelief, she said nothing but her face crumpled and she began to cry silently. In my entire life to that point, I had never (that I remember) seen my Mother cry, and it shocked me. Sadly, it also triggered me, and rather than going in for a hug (but then, we didn't do that in our family), instead I started shouting at her:

"What are you crying for? You don't know how lucky you are! You have everything!"

I believe I might have gone on to say worse; it's all lost to my unconscious mind now.

What has stuck with me though, is that intense feeling of scorn, that somehow I felt was appropriate in my 15-year-old brain. Scorn for the crying, scorn for the display of non-standard emotion (and even of initial emotional-limbo), scorn for not maintaining the *status quo* and the 'brave face' expected of Mothers everywhere; scorn for daring to reveal the tiniest fragment of herself and truth in that moment. I was perplexed at this impromptu uncovering, and I think it scared me.

Because who was my Mother, really? In that moment she might as well have cried out that she was gay, or had suffered a miscarriage, or her best friend had died: the result was the same. I realised I had no idea who my mum was, on any tangible level. Until that moment, her entire identity to me was her title and role as a parent, as a Mother.

I never did find out why my mum was crying that day. And I never asked. It might have been menopausal hormones raging around, and the stress of living in a house with a raging-hormonal teen at the same time. The point is, our society teaches us not to care – and moreover, to be surprised and scornful at Mothers who 'break down,' even in the sanctity of their own homes.

I have done my fair share of crying as a Mother myself, since – that's for sure.

When I think of the role of Mother in the patriarchal era, it is always in this way. We treat Mother Earth, the Divine Feminine aspect, and feminine energy the same: what is expected and deemed 'appropriate' is a stripped-down and manipulated version of her fullness. She is here very much, to serve. We gaslight and demonise her truths and her fundamental power. And we scorn her emotion, her felt-senses, her embodied wisdom.

When we deny, neglect and suppress these uniquely feminine energies and qualities, we directly cut ourselves off from our own nourishment. We become plants that have used weedkiller on our own soil.

Who is Mother Earth – and Why is She Crying?

We have forced ourselves to dissociate from her, and so we no longer know who or what she is. All we 'know' is our scorn, our overriding pride in our own intelligence and power, and our absolute belief we are right and she is wrong. All of our systems and structures – government, schooling, judicial and even health – are based on the premise of control, external motivation, suppression of symptoms and punishment; the rooted, life-giving principles of 'nourishment' don't even get a look-in.

As above, so below. As within, so without. We are walking microcosms of the world we have created, and vice versa. If a rash appears, we want to smother it in a steroid cream. If a child is 'difficult' in class, we place them in detention and seek to enforce the message of their wrongness. If a forest lies in the path of a planned convenience route, we raze it down and concrete over it.

We have created arbitrary, yet rigid, timetables for every minute of every day of every week of every year, in which we are pressed to fit or suffer the consequences. 9 to 5, 40 hours, five bank holidays, Christmas and New Year if you're lucky. From the earliest age, our children are coerced into seats and promised rewards if they sit there all day long and don't disrupt the lesson-giving. Attendance is mandatory, and if it drops below 90% the whole families in trouble.

We are moulded into boxes of expectation and life-goals which serve the productivity-based capitalist regime. From infancy we are taught to idolise service to an existing system – lawyer, bank clerk, doctor – and push everything outside of those boxes firmly into the 'hobby' category. Money is conditioned as our primary motivation; our very *raison-d'être*. For without money, what is life? What is left? So ingrained and thorough is this conditioning, most of us can't even begin to imagine such a world.

The saddest part of this is that accessing and continuing to develop our *wholeness* – even simply our *whole brain* through increased right-brain activities and their strengthening connection back to the left brain via the corpus callossum – really is our basic right and need. And yet it has been systematically and systemically castrated for centuries.

The life-giving and soul-nourishing act of honouring our whole brain, our whole physical body, our whole energetic body and the wholeness of our multi-sensorial interdependent connection to all that surrounds us – seen and unseen – is categorically what makes us entire, unbroken human beings.

And what of our wisdom? Our gut instinct, our *knowing*? This almost always becomes conscious when we become Mothers (if not before). I've yet to meet a Mum who doesn't have a story of 'just knowing' something was about to happen, or wasn't quite right, or they were urged to action in a specific moment. And though they couldn't have reasoned why, they _knew_ – and they have been forever thankful since, for trusting that knowing. Sitting in a doctor's office, I've had this knowing scorned (and even shamed) out of me again and again and again. Replace the doctor with 'well-meaning' policemen, schoolteachers, welfare officers, council officials, and the story is exactly the same: our wisdom is a base threat to their systems, and so it is routinely smothered.

Who IS Mother? And why *is* she crying?

I often wonder who I would be now if I had not had children. I'm sure every Mother feels this at times. And I declare it here now in the fullness of what it takes within our society to make the transition to Motherhood, and to persist in the vastly under-supported journey of becoming, and growing, as Mothers through all the ages and levels of our dependents.

It is far from easy, especially as the village it takes has been removed. In its place, we grapple with authority figures who don't know us, and are routinely batted around the many hallowed halls of child-centred medical and social pathology.

There is no heart.

There is no nurture.

There is no empathy, no real compassion, no connected understanding.

There is no allowance of multiple, layered truths, of nuance.

There is no bigger picture; nor honed-in personalisation.

There is no sacred space; no sanctity for our wholeness.

In those first months – years – of being a new mum, I completely lost myself. I didn't know who I was or what in hell I'd unwittingly signed up to. My baby cried constantly, but no expert or authority figure showed any interest; everything was pathologically 'normal' and that was that. Mothering, I quickly discovered, was also its own unique form of competition – not just for the snappiest babygros and trendiest carriers, but for how *good* your baby was. Sleeping, not crying, putting on the 'right' amount of weight, eating at exactly six months and weaning without effort. And of course, as Mums we pitted against each other for all of it, and more _ for losing the 'baby weight,' for getting back to work and plunging back into our sex lives. For somehow treating this life-changing and ongoing 'event' as if we'd done no more than break an arm.

It's no wonder that in my firstborn's early months on this planet, I wanted to erase my own life from it. At the time, we lived near Pontcysyllte Aqueduct, and more than once, my husband had to wrestle me back from the edge. I share this without shame or fear, as I can now see the raw and gruesome truth of my situation at that time – and equally, of almost every new Mother I've known.

Our Mother Energy is crying out to us. She desperately needs us to reconnect with her, on every level – for our own wellbeing *and* that of our communities, and our planet. But what will this really take?

Thankfully, I believe the transition has already begun. Women are speaking out more and more about the injustices and inequalities that have been assumed for too long to simply be our lot in life. During the pandemic, it became crystal clear to us that, for example, our menfolk could stay at home and share the chaotic juggling act of childcare and house admin: something women have typically taken on by default for centuries, despite *also* having a job/running a business, etc.

Slowly, yet exponentially, we are waking up. We are creating and following movements in which we now honour our womb-cycles, our energy rhythms, and our creative ebbs and flows. We are (almost en masse now!) tuning into the energies of the Earth, of our bodies and energy spheres, and of the collective on a daily basis. We are doing our own shadow work, including that related to the ancestral Mother Wound. And we are noticing, bit by bit, how all of this feels within our bodies – as traumatic trace-memories of each generation of women that went before us, and all they endured.

We are healing ourselves and our future generations. We are rebirthing our wholeness.

And as we create these shifts back towards our feminine energy; as we *own* this energy as powerful and intrinsic to our being, so we also begin to heal the Great Mother herself.

The imbalance of wounded masculine over wounded feminine has been present too long. In this great healing phase, we are not only beginning to balance the scales, equally we are unwrapping the deep wounds of both and lovingly tending to the root causes – finally. In this process, we begin to understand on an experiential level that there is no linear path from A-Z. Logic cannot give us the definitive answers. Our bodies and energies hold the potential to communicate far more information and wisdom than our entrained minds. Honouring and following our energetic rhythms makes all the difference to how we feel *and* the outcome. Being a woman in this world *need not equate* to having our very essence and intrinsic power squashed: all it takes is for us to wake up and stand up.

Knowing the Mother Energy means knowing and understanding the very roots of our existence, and our own incredible power as creators, whether male, female or trans. Being willing to pause and truly *listen* to her in this pivotal point, in time means listening to our own fullness and wholeness. And then, connecting with genuine, felt empathy for her tears allows our own smothered wounds to begin healing.

We are all in this together. And we have the potential to fully embody and express the expansive, potent creatrix energy of the Mother *if we choose to do so.*

Imagine *that* world, for a moment.

She is waiting for us.

MOTHERHOOD ENERGY AND THE CHILDFREE ROAD LESS TRAVELLED

By Jennifer Flint

Until my early forties, I was always ambivalent about Motherhood.

My earliest memory of a conversation about having children was age 17 at sixth form college. Three friends and I were discussing what our potential futures might hold and, despite being an overweight, moody Goth at the time, I was apparently going to become a 'business --woman' – even though I'm sure none of us knew what this meant and can only guess it was based on some modest success as an Avon lady.

I was also, accurately, the only one predicted not to have children.

Over the years, I became accustomed to being the odd one out as a childfree woman. On the outside looking in.

Every time I met someone new and they asked, 'Do you have children?'

Every time I found myself marooned inside a conversation about how to get kids to eat their greens. And every time I stopped to think about how everyone around me was consumed with raising their families.

Being the 'other' was simply like static in the background of my inner life.

Unexpectedly, everything changed on the evening of my Mother's sixty-fifth birthday, at the exact moment I finally thought I had all my shit together at the beginning of my fabulous forties!

I had secured a big promotion at work, my husband and I had successfully navigated a rocky patch in our marriage, and we had just finished renovating our house. All I would have to do from here on in, I naively believed, was keep all the plates spinning smoothly!

My husband and I were lying on the kitchen floor after everyone had left the birthday party, sipping champagne and admiring how our new skylights elevated the ceiling, when he looked tenderly into my eyes and said, "Babe ... I would really love us to have a baby."

Something about the way he said it, with a look of such love, pierced me with a single clean incision. In that instant, I had a stunning realisation. I had *assumed* I would not have children but had not wholeheartedly *decided*: age 41, the question of whether or not I would have children was about to be made *for* me, not *by* me.

As an independent, educated woman, committed to living in an intentional way, I suddenly felt that failing to come off the fence of my ambivalence to make a wholehearted and definitive choice would be a disservice to myself. A clear decision would ensure no loose ends were left dangling in my psyche; the psychological equivalent of sewing my tubes together with nice, neat stitches, making a sturdy seam between a future childfree life and the fictional one in which

I became a Mother. That way, I would not be tempted to pick at the frayed edge of regret in later years.

I needed, in other words, to say a 'Hell yes', or a 'Hell no,' to Motherhood.

The following day, I sat down and made a list of pros and cons, assuming the whole issue would be quickly and efficiently resolved with my usual application of logical reasoning.

I remember smiling to myself, feeling as though this exercise was the passing out parade for my midlife upgrade.

To my shock and horror, I discovered a seed of doubt and tumbled down a dark, existential rabbit hole into Maybe-Baby Hell where I waged war with myself, plagued 24/7 by the same questions going round and round ...

Why is something so instinctive to others so elusive to me?

Why am I so closed off to my own knowing?

Is there something missing in me?

Am I selfish?

What if I regret not having children?

After three months of writing multiple pros and cons lists (desperately hoping that if I did it enough times I would have a breakthrough!) I exhausted the limits of rational decision making and began to explore other means to break through my deadlock.

I interviewed a friend of a friend who had been ambivalent and then came off the fence in favour of having a baby.

I read several books.

I delved into the world of online blogs exploring Motherhood and non-motherhood from three hundred-and-sixty-degree angles.

When none of this worked, I became increasingly desperate and, on the recommendation of a friend, tried bodywork therapy to get out of my exhausted head and into my body, which subsequently led to a course of psychotherapy.

Finally, nine months after that kitchen-floor moment, I heard a quiet whisper from my heart, and she told me to come off the pill. Not because I had decided I wanted to get pregnant per se, but more because I was finally tuning in to my much neglected intuition and this is what she invited me to do.

To my surprise, I fell pregnant within a couple of months.

Deep down however, I knew something was off and had a miscarriage after ten weeks.

"At least we know we can get pregnant now," said my husband. "We can try again."

I remember nodding and agreeing but feeling my words sounded oddly hollow.

About three months later, I was about to leave the bathroom, when I noticed my body had stopped in front of the bathroom cabinet. It was a peculiar feeling, as my body seemed to have done this in the absence of any instruction from my brain.

I felt like I was observing myself from a distance as I saw my hand grab the cabinet door, with such force I almost ripped it off its hinges, and watched as my hands scrambled to find my contraceptive pills, popped open a foil window, and threw a tiny lilac pill down my throat.

I swallowed with a loud, dramatic gulp.

And then I heard a voice in my head.

A clear, calm voice.

"*Motherhood is not my path,*" it said.

I felt the truth of this statement simultaneously in every cell of my body. A clear, unequivocal, 'HELL NO' to Motherhood.

"Now THAT was a decision," I said aloud, as I stood rooted to the spot, feeling a tingling energy all round my body.

"*Now what?*" came the voice in my head again.

A few months later, through a series of serendipitous events, I was led to a tiny Tibetan Buddhist Island on the West Coast of Scotland called Holy Isle. Honestly, I didn't really know why I was there, I just had a feeling that I was searching for something in the wake of slamming the door to Motherhood firmly shut.

Within a few hours of arriving, I met a childfree woman the same age as me who has become a dear friend. It was her second time on the island, having first found Holy Isle a few years earlier when she was searching for a place to 'grieve for her Mother' who had sadly died of cancer.

As soon as I heard those words, tears of recognition began dripping onto my lap.

I knew why I was there.

I had come to grieve for Motherhood.

My friend and I spent a lot of time together during the three days I was there.

During one conversation, she said that whilst she was at peace with not having children, she had always felt a sense of having what she called 'Motherhood energy' inside her ... a compelling urge to nurture and give birth to things outside of herself.

For her, this was an energy she expressed through growing plants and making herbal remedies. As soon as she uttered those words, I knew this was something alive inside me too, so when I left the island my quest to understand and manifest 'Motherhood energy' in my own life began.

I started by exploring the possibility of re-training as a psychotherapist. I was a successful but unfulfilled HR Director at the time and felt attracted towards this kind of deeper one-to-one work.

Perhaps, I thought, my expression of 'Motherhood Energy' might be holding space for emotional and psychological healing through therapy. I even attended an open evening for a four-year diploma programme, effectively pressing my face up against the proverbial shop window, but I didn't feel a, 'Hell yes,' in my body, so I let the opportunity go and decided to wait.

Next, inspired by having attended a couple of courses in London, I began exploring the possibility of re-kindling an abandoned dream of writing a book inspired by my father's early life as a lighthouse keeper. Excitedly, I started to make headway but after six months fell out of the saddle for the umpteenth time, knocked off the creative writing horse by intense imposter syndrome.

So I did what any self-respecting, A-type, controlling perfectionist does ... I buried myself in work!

A year later, one bleak winter's night, I had a dark night of the soul.

I was driving home from the office after being kicked out by the cleaners at 7:00pm.

Again.

The car windscreen wipers were working on full tilt and my body was tense, leaning forward. It was difficult to see ahead through the pelting rain.

Suddenly I heard a clear, calm voice in my head.

"If you just did this ..." it said flashing an image of me wrenching the steering wheel hard to the right "...you could have a crash, and die, and then it would all be over."

"Yeah," came another voice, "But my mam would kill me."

"Fair point," came the reply.

The following morning, I was driving to head office on my usual route. As I approached a level crossing, the lights began flashing indicating the gates were about to close, and the voice came again.

"If you just drove onto the railway line now and stopped the car, the train would hit you, and you would die, then it would all be over."

"Yeah," came a reply, "But the poor train driver would probably be traumatised for life and might never be able to work again."

"Fair point" came another reply.

A few weeks later, I arrived for my first counselling session. I had almost cancelled, but left it too late to do so without seeming rude, so reluctantly I attended the appointment.

I sat on a low armchair in a beige room opposite a woman who looked a little like Jilly Cooper, assuming it would be my first and last visit.

I was a senior leader with a demanding job, doing the most intense and complex project of my career, working long hours, with no end in sight: of course I was going to be feeling stressed and overwhelmed. "*So what?*" I thought. "*I just need to let off a bit of steam, learn an extra strategy for staying resilient. Job done.*"

Except it wasn't.

A tiny tug brought me back to that small room for the second time. A faint feeling that there was something else beneath the surface, and there was digging to be done.

By the fifth session, the proverbial spade hit a hard floor.

We had reached the bottom.

I wasn't stressed.

I was grieving.

"Three years ago," I explained as I juddered to a halt after crying for fifty minutes, "I closed the door to Motherhood and chose not to have children. I am at peace with my decision but have been left with this feeling of having Motherhood Energy inside me ... a yearning for something to be expressed and birthed through me. The problem is, I haven't done anything about it. Instead, I've buried myself in work, and I feel like this energy is metastasising."

Six months later I attended a retreat back on Holy Isle. I had agreed to go along with a friend who said she wanted some company and, not needing much excuse to revisit my special island, I said yes without even knowing what the programme was about.

The beginning of the advert read as follows ...

This retreat explores how to fearlessly embrace our Shadow Side with compassionate acceptance and step into the power of our fullest potential.

The Shadow is made up of all that we hide from others: our shame, our fears, our psychological wounds, but also our golden potential, our blinding beauty and our hidden talents. It is a huge source of power and creativity but until we bring it into the light this power will remain untapped and our full potential unreached.

This retreat offers a set of powerful practices including shamanic mask and mirror work, Jungian inquiry and Tibetan Buddhist meditations to transform shame into acceptance and fear into love.

It turned out to be the most powerful and transformative personal development experience of my life. By the time I left, I knew something profound had shifted.

Within a matter of weeks, I was facilitating my first group coaching session for a long time – volunteering on a Sunday to help out a friend called Tracey.

My group consisted of five middle-aged women and Tracey's daughter, Jess.

At the time, Jess was three months away from her eighteenth birthday. Since the age of ten, a rare brain disease had dominated her life, so through her childhood and teen years Jess had endured a great deal of stress and uncertainty about the future, compounded by frustration at not being listened to by the medical profession and feeling '*like a lab rat*' as they scratched their heads trying to diagnose her illness.

This condition had affected all areas of Jess's life – her friendships, family, appearance, physical and mental health and her dreams for the future. Some of the lowest points included becoming suicidal in reaction to medication, being hi-jacked by a seizure that left her blind in one eye, and dropping out of full-time education.

During that first group coaching session, Jess told us her story. "*I have all of this unprocessed emotion and I don't know what to do with it,*" she said. "*I feel like turning eighteen is intensifying everything for me. I have this drive to use what has happened to me to make a difference. I can feel it welling up inside, and I need to find some direction.*"

Listening to Jess, it struck me that what she needed was a rite of passage. Six months earlier, at the end of my counselling sessions, I'd been led to a weekend course to train as an independent celebrant without knowing why I was there, other than it felt mysteriously connected to this idea of 'Motherhood Energy.' I had yet to perform a ceremony, but felt compelled to reach out to Jess to pitch an idea.

As a party was already planned to celebrate her eighteenth birthday, what if we designed a bespoke 'Coming Of Age' ceremony to take place in the venue earlier that day? I suggested this could provide a way to help her release the grief she was carrying, and to mindfully set intentions about how she might use her experience to forge a positive pathway into adulthood.

To my delight, and also terror, Jess said yes and our creative partnership began.

At our first design meeting, I explained the basic scaffolding of a ceremony and we began to play with ideas. "*I feel like so much of my childhood was taken away from me,*" Jess said. "*I want to re-discover the little girl I lost along the way. I want this ceremony to be as creative as I was when I was a kid.*"

This statement formed our guiding objective and as the creative process unfolded, Jess grew bolder; both in terms of the rituals she wanted to include and the messages she wished to convey. "*Losing my sight has really made me see things differently,*" she told me when we met to discuss the first draft. "*It's like, I have this heightened sense of the joy of being alive. It's made me feel that I want to live life to the fullest, to remember every day to stop and really look at the world around me, take it all in, and be grateful for everything I have. So, I want this ceremony to offer this gift of awareness to the people I really care about.*"

Each time we spoke, I came away feeling inspired, and committed to finding the courage to be the celebrant Jess deserved.

Seven family members and a friend attended the final ceremony. After a processional piece of music, we opened with a blessing. In turn, Jess's mum, dad, sister and grandmothers stepped forward and lit candles to represent the pain of letting go; the courage to face challenges; shared memories; and unconditional love.

Jess also lit a candle to represent childhood and we played a second piece of music, which Jess chose to evoke the joy and wonderment of her youth, before she stepped forward to deliver a eulogy for childhood, in her own words. She marked closure by placing a single red rose on a small homemade coffin draped with black velvet.

We moved into the next section of the ceremony via a third piece of music, which represented the threshold between childhood and adulthood. The soundtrack also acted as a prelude to Jess making vows to her future self, which she read whilst standing in front of a mirror – chosen as a symbol of self-knowledge to represent a gateway between the Jess of today, and the Jess of tomorrow.

After making her commitments we enjoyed a fourth piece of music, which Jess chose to embody the sound and spirit of her future, and transitioned us into the final stage of the ceremony.

This final part was dedicated to gathering resources for Jess to take forward on her journey, and naming and letting go of whatever she needed to leave behind. We did this by inviting each guest to come forward and share a meaningful item they wanted to put into a Memory Box – bestowing a gift that would provide strength and nourishment for Jess in the future.

This was followed by a Phoenix Bowl ritual whereby I invited Jess to leave behind something that she wished to release, bidding it goodbye with love, peace and acceptance.

Finally, we closed with Jess and her Mum sipping from a Quaich Cup, to symbolise their love for, and confidence in each other, before Jess blew out the candles.

Jess later described the ceremony as 'a spiritual awakening' through which she was able to recover and redefine buried parts of herself. "After the ceremony, I felt refreshed and new. Now, I feel awakened and like I'm living an authentic life and proudly owning it."

And Tracey said, "*I listened to my precious daughter talk about her struggles, but also how they have shaped her, made her feisty and resilient. In that ceremony I emotionally let go of my little girl who needed her Mam, and I welcomed the woman ... I knew my time to let go of the loving reins was here and it allowed me to step back and watch my daughter take charge of her own life and health. We celebrated our family, the tough times we have encountered, and the love that has kept us together. It was beautiful, emotional, and life affirming. I watched my daughter walk across the bridge to adulthood ... It was a beautiful way to celebrate Jess as a woman, and how we all move together watching her grow further.*"

It turned out that Jess's ceremony was also a 'rite of passage' for me.

A few months later, I had another stunning moment of clarity and resigned from my HR Director role. I had no plan, no savings, and no new job to go to, but I was now in touch with my intuition and trusted myself to follow it.

What unfolded in the wake of this bold move was beyond my wildest dreams.

My organisation created a two-year fixed term role, three days per week, doing impactful coaching and leadership development work with Tracey that I absolutely loved, and for which we won a prestigious national award. At the end of the contract, I left my corporate career on a high and set up my own business at the end of 2021.

Whilst working part-time, I also got back on to the writing saddle, just as lockdown happened and joined a mini 'Write That Book' pop up group which led to me writing and publishing (much to my surprise!) my debut novel called *Wild Egg – A story of one woman's search for her childfree life* which (thrillingly) officially launched in July 2022 and is now available to buy on Amazon and via all independent book shops.

Following the ceremony, I also became officially bestowed with the honorary title 'The Other Mother' by Jess and Tracey, which has brought so much joy to my life – especially when I took Jess for her first visit to magical Holy Isle in summer 2019 – and have continued to support her as she has embarked on a degree in psychology. Giving her a signed copy of my book a few days ago, which is dedicated to her, along with two other special women, was a moment I will treasure for the rest of my life – especially as Jess is now considering writing her own story one day.

Looking back at my journey, from that kitchen-floor moment, to writing this chapter as part of a fabulous and inspiring collaboration of Wake-Up-Mother women, I now see the extent to which I had been programmed to believe that not wanting children was something to be ashamed of; something abnormal that made me 'lesser than.'

And ... please excuse my French ... but I no longer believe this crock of shit!

I am older and wiser now. I was 41 when I was in the dark pit of ambivalence and I'm going on 51 now.

I now understand that a big part of what I wrestled with back then, was pronatalist conditioning. 'Pronatalism' is a powerful ideology which is pro-birth, encourages reproduction and glorifies the role of parenthood.[1] It is a cultural belief which pervades all forms of social conditioning – right from the fairy tales we read as little girls that invariably cast women without children as wicked stepmothers, crazy cat ladies, or baby-eating witches; to the recent calls in the mainstream media to tax people without children, or ban people with children from going abroad in the summer holidays.[2]

I have the greatest of respect for anyone who chooses to have children. I also passionately believe that becoming a biological Mother is only ONE rite of passage on our journey into becoming the fullest expression of ourselves, not THE way which it is so often framed as being.

There are many ways in which we can come full circle as a woman. I took a different path and I am deeply at peace with my choice. I have absolutely no regrets whatsoever and enjoy a rich and meaningful life blessed with many women who are Mothers and many who – like me – are childfree by choice, or childless by circumstance.

In the post-Roe vs Wade landscape I believe more than ever, we must fight for the right to be sovereign over our own bodies, and to be trusted and equally respected in making choices that are right for us and aligned to our deepest truth. And, as this collaborative book so beautifully demonstrates, there is so much more that unites us than divides us.

1 Laura Carroll The Baby Matrix
2 Both suggestions that appeared in The Sunday Times and The Telegraph in July 2022.

HOW QIGONG HELPED ME FIND SELF-CARE IN SINGLE MOTHERHOOD

By Clara Apollo

Before I got pregnant with my only son, I trained to be a nurse, being fascinated about how bodies worked with a keen interest in health. However, I really struggled working in the NHS and found it to be a predominately disease-based service.

Where was the health?

As training continued, I became more and more sensitive to the trauma that illness puts people through and wondered why there seemed to be so little incentive towards preventative healthcare.

At school, both human biology and art were my favourite subjects and during Sixth Form, I'd steered more towards creative expression, but my parents had their minds set on me becoming a nurse. I was hatching another plan. Soon after qualifying as a registered nurse, I was free of parental shackles and quit nursing, getting a place at a London art college to study printed textiles and costume design. Result!

After the degree show, I was free to pursue being a creative performer and formed a glam-punk party group with my then boyfriend, creating off-the-wall outfits for our band members whilst earning money as a costume designer and childminder during the day.

This was a hedonist rocket blast of creative madness, involving a variety of personal relationships and wild party behaviour. As fun as this was, I knew I couldn't keep the pace going and anyway, I felt empty. There was something more brewing for me, when I had an epiphany, on stage.

Bedecked in silver space-glam-punk wear and ridiculous platform soles, I launched a handful of glitter onto the 200+ grinning audience. Watching the light catching the sparkling motes as they blessed the spectators, came the dawning of a deeper thought – and time seemed to stand still. In that space, dropped the realisation that I was in a privileged position, yet all I was doing was dressing up, twirling props, messing with lyrics and chucking glitter about. Yes, I was fortunate to be in a band with a bunch of great musicians and friends, but there was something else I was here to offer the world.

What was this?

I didn't know at the time, but I did feel things were on the change and wondered how I could shift my trajectory?

Then I fell pregnant. A perfect 'accident'.

I'd always wanted to be a Mother and would gravitate towards children, adoring how they explore through play so freely. Having maverick tendencies, I ruled out any conventional routes to parenting. I had already experienced two terminations, the last one taking me through a deep grieving process. I had promised myself that if I got pregnant again, I would see it through.

Here was my opportunity.

I met my son's father whilst auditioning a new bass guitarist for the band and had an instant attraction. I lived in a small flat in North London, he was squatting around and about, so I invited him to move in and within six months of our first meeting, I fell pregnant. We married five months before the birth. He was American and needed a visa to be able to stay in the UK.

I felt it was my destiny – it was a choice point for sure, although a deeper sense at my core was apprehensive about our coupling. There was something not chiming true, and yet I could sense the powerful new soul inside me yearning to be born and wanting me to be their Mum.

Becoming Pregnant was an Act of Self-Care

Interestingly, I found it easy to give up dodgy habits; having another being reliant on me for their health spurred me into action to take care of my own. I continued performing with the band until a month before the birth and could feel him moving in time to the music we played. I generally loved how having a swollen belly felt. The honour of growing a new being inside me was a sacred act. Later my Qigong training illustrated why.

Our bellies house an energy centre called Dantien, which exists co-spatially with the sacral chakra. This is a truly magical centre of balance, vitality and creation. It's a gathering place for the highest energies of heaven, earth and the elements to meet in alchemy. This resource gives a grounding place for the heart and soul to feel safe in the body. It is also a portal to other dimensions.

Wow!

How I'd wished to have known that way back then. There are some beautiful movements and meditations to nourish growing babes. All I gave mine was (mostly) soothing conversations, music, song and a happy hand on the tum!

My birthing plan insisted on having no midwife students present and only in a hospital if I could bring a birthing pool. I remember fighting for that self-care right, and chose a wonderful woman to be there as the 'pool attendant' and female companion alongside the midwife.

I had a natural birth, 13 hours from early morning to early evening, using breathwork with gas and air. I was bereft that I could not get in the pool until a certain dilation as it was too relaxing and boy it was. To go from 'I can't do this' to slipping into the perfect temperature of water, utterly soothed my system.

I've learned that adrenaline production is drastically reduced when the skin is immersed in water; maybe this is something to do with a return to a sublime holding in the amniotic fluid of gestation?

Once in the water, I regrouped into feeling like a whole person again; the water connected with its sensory magic on my skin and I became more present.

Due to complications, it was recommended I climb out to actually give birth. It was good I had made the choice to not have a student deliver me, as at the pushing stage, my midwife looked directly into my eyes and said:

"The umbilical cord is wound twice around his neck, I will have to cut it before you push, which means when I say push, you really do have to push him out."

It all felt part of the process, however risky in retrospect. We worked together and delivered him safely – it was only later that she said that it had been touch and go. I wonder if there had been a student that the outcome may not have been so positive. I'd followed my gut instinct for self-care during labour, yes!!

That he was a boy made me laugh. I'd been so convinced he was a girl – maybe it's because I am. His gender seemed somewhat irrelevant at that moment, as did a name. I was absolutely elated at seeing his brilliant deep wise eyes for the first time, so amazed at the whole intense process we'd been engrossed in together, as we tickled him into breathing.

The Motherhood Pledge

After a few stitches and weighing him up, the staff left the room and my husband went to call our families. I was alone with my dearest babe for the first time with him outside of my body. I felt energetically massive, like I'd achieved the greatest act of my life and made a pledge to him in that moment, whilst he slept blissfully after all that birthing effort.

Sensing the presence of my Grandmothers, I felt the commonality of childbirth through the ages and pledged unwavering responsibility for him for at least the next 18 years with the best care I could muster. Of course, a Mother's love never ends, but the responsibility shifts as the apron strings lengthen, twist and turn! I was blissfully unaware at that time to bless myself and to remember that self-care would help me too, supporting my care of him. Those lessons were to come.

I discharged us that very evening, despite hospital protocols and we took him back home proudly to begin our new life as a family.

Suddenly everything changed. Priorities shifted to 'baby first' every time, of course. He slept alongside our bed in his own cot for ease of night time feeds. That first morning of waking up and him being there, outside of me, yet still such a part of me, is such a precious memory. Sometimes during the night feeds, I was so weary, I'd be holding my arms tightly in the optimal position to ensure he was held at the right level for feeding. I know now a better use of pillows would have helped. I didn't know that breastfeeding like this would cause RSI, a painful inflammation on both my forearms, causing a weakness for many years which would later become the cause of my change of career. further down the line.

Reclaiming My Playtime

About eight weeks after I gave birth, one of my favourite bands was coming to town. I knew that if it was at all possible, I wanted to go to the gig. It was the B-52s and I was a big fan! I even had the ideal post-pregnancy outfit lined up – a purple velvet V-neck tunic mini-dress with a ruffled white blouse.

But who could I leave my precious baby with? My husband was well up for going to see this band too and none of my other friends were baby savvy. Then I remembered the woman who lived next door to where I was when my lad was conceived. Her place was a shared squat (there were many around in the late 1980's), and she was there with her young daughter Faith, so I knew that she was cool with babies. I questioned whether it was the right environment for him to stay without me for the first time. I tuned into my heart and trusted that the memory of conversations I'd had with her were from the place of the wise intuitive parent, although with an inspiringly unorthodox approach.

I asked if she would babysit my little one for a few hours on the proposed evening if he was well fed, sleepy and ready to be coddled. I was expressing milk too, so a couple of little bottles went with him, and so it was set. I fed him before putting on my glad rags and trusted that it would be fine.

Putting on my make-up in the mirror I recognised playtime Clara was still there, although with fresh Motherhood eyes. I reclaimed a key part of who I am, alongside a newly developing side of being a responsible Mumma for my dear baby boy.

I'm not going to lie, it was very difficult leaving him there when it came to it. The wrench was massive and I felt super selfish, but my husband said;

"He's okay, he's safe, we can do this."

I had the best time, surrendering to the incredible performances, singing and dancing along. By the end of the gig my breasts were exploding, leaking into my purple velvet dress!

A new experience on embarrassment. I stuffed some tissues down my burgeoning bra and said;

"We have to go now and collect our son."

When we picked him up, he was sound asleep. He'd been absolutely fine. I was so, so grateful. Following my wishes whilst taking care of his needs showed me that there were ways of weaving both – being practical and trusting in my intuitive Motherhood heart.

Sacred Endings and New Beginnings

Due to the RSI, I had to stop nursing him at six months old.

I didn't really know what to do with the continued pain and eventually found a short article in the National Childbirth Trust magazine (no Internet in 1990), suggesting that there may also be a hormonal predisposition which, when coupled with strain of the forearm, would produce the pain. The only path to take was to stop breastfeeding him. He was six months old, hungry and I was kind of done.

Yes, it was sad to stop that bonding time with him.

I consciously planned the last feed with a poignant sadness, alongside the joy that I'd actually been able to feed him up until now; my little boobs worked! This also honoured a deep need in me to reinstate a better level of self-care.

When my lad was just over two years old, I split from my husband. It had been a marriage largely of convenience. I was sure that I could make being a single mum work, as I lived in a neighbourhood with many children. My son continued to see his Dad every other weekend and still has a strong connection with him.

Determined not to return to the punishing levels of creative output pre-birth, I would still sometimes find myself working on costumes into the night, to be there for him during the day. It was intense and I managed it, just. I remember once getting a photo of me holding a candle in the middle with both ends burning, thinking it was funny – albeit slightly hysterically! I had no idea what I was doing to my personal energy. All I knew was that as long as I had good food, a comfy bed, high grade coffee and weed, I would find a balance!

What I was about to learn blew these unsustainable methods out of the water.

When the RSI reappeared due to an intense period of stitching, a Dad of one of my son's young friends offered me some healing. He was trained in shiatsu, energy healing and Qigong. During the first session, he pronounced that my prenatal qi was shot!

Instantly questions popped up:

What on earth is prenatal qi? And is this serious?

Qigong energy cultivation wisdom is a practice I was about to be introduced to. Let me first share with you this key factor to personal energy management.

Prenatal qi, or Primordial Essence, is the term given to a bequeathing of vital life force energy from both your parents before birth. From the Chinese Medicine perspective, this is considered to be the most important factor in one's health and vitality, as when you use it up, you die.

Scary stuff, until you find out there is an antidote.

We can choose to either nurture this primal life-force energy, or use it up.

I do wish I'd known this foundational fact before proudly burning that candle at both ends!

I had no idea that my lifestyle choices of late night work and play would have deeper significance on my fundamental energy stores. No wonder I was waking up after a night's sleep feeling exhausted. It was my prenatal qi stores in full-on depletion, a.k.a. burnout.

So yes, this was serious.

This Essential Essence is stored around the Kidney area, and is released as and when required to support growth and development, including reproduction. The Kidneys are also considered to be the root of the Yin and Yang energies in the body, our innate balancing system. That is why it is important we keep the small of our back covered and warm.

It made a big difference to me when I ceased wearing crop tops and kept my middle warm. In oriental cultures they have a garment called a Haramaki – belly wrap – to maintain core warmth and improve blood circulation.

The Healer Dad went on to say that there are ways to restore this life force quotient, the most effective of which is Qigong. Would I like to give it a go?

Well, yes, I guess. If there was an antidote to this self-sabotaging behaviour, bring it on! But what on earth was Qigong? I'd never heard of it. He told me it was at the root of Tai Chi and other Martial Arts, which woke me right up into a; "Hell yes!"

If this practice was underpinning these traditional paths, what could it do for me?

Rekindling Self-Care with Qigong

What this also gave me was a priority remit to put my needs on the same level as my son's. He was around five years old and luckily a dear friend, who lived in the flat below, agreed to babysit so I could go to practice. It was so divinely set up, although I had no conscious awareness of such energies at play back then.

The Healer Dad invited me into his Qigong class, just a short walk from my home. Not knowing quite what I was letting myself in for, I felt the urge to explore how to heal myself with meditational movement and entered this new Qi space with my curiosity cap on.

It was like walking through a portal.

I looked at the assembled group and wondered:

What is this?

Why are all the participants standing still?

I found a place and joined in. We were guided into an optimal posture and I landed, somewhat irritated, into the present moment, not a place I'd noticed much before. Remembering my curiosity cap, I became mesmerised by just **how** I was standing: where my weight was, how the soles of my feet were in direct connection with the power of the planet while my crown was being drawn up to the stars, and how my spine naturally lengthened between these two places.

Was this the 'Now' that I'd scurried past, running headlong into the future?

This was way before mindfulness became mainstream. Qigong offered me a massive perspective shift for the very much better. I found the space I'd longed for. It was in me all along.

The Qi invitation is to just notice. Open your awareness into how you feel. Listen in to your system's subtle – or not so subtle – ways of communicating and tune in with yourself, with compassion, curiosity and kindness.

Personal Forgiveness

Oh my, I was tense! All the years of costume making was stuck in my neck and shoulders, with the RSI lodged in my forearms along with lower back stiffness. It made me sad and angry how I had mistreated myself all these years. Uncomfy feelings that had been suppressed were surfacing now to be cleared out. I was remorseful, apologising to my body for inflicting this disrespect for so long. I made another pledge to take better care, which would require a radical shift of self-management, and that didn't happen overnight.

Qi Moves for the First Time

After the initial standing structure was set up, we moved into a set of joint opening movements, circling the hips, turning the spine and rotating the shoulders. One exercise, the 'Monkey Forward Bend', has become a favourite. I particularly like it as an anti-gravity antidote to ease my neck. This is better for my shoulder needs than the pressure of yoga's shoulder stand and is still a daily go-to move for me.

We then got into a 'form' to move the Qi around, activating meridian lines up and down the legs. I knew this was aligned with the wisdom of acupuncture and shiatsu. It felt good to clear out old energetic waste deep down through the roots we'd anchored previously into the Earth.

This intentional act creates space to gather up fresh vitality to the magical place of abundance in our bellies I mentioned earlier, the Dantien.

I think of this place as being like a personal rechargeable battery unit that can be replenished with specific moves and intentions.

As the session continued, it became apparent that the sturdy posture facilitates the upper body's ease of movement. I loved the rekindling of ballet-style moves, arms gliding through the air, undulating, rotating and swirling effortlessly, enjoying movement for movement's sake. As my joints freed up, some actions had me landing my hands on the body with percussive taps, slaps or strokes, like a self-massage to clear and refresh. After the session, I floated home, snuggled with my lad and had the best night's sleep for an age.

Here is where my relationship with parenting shifted. I began to look at self-care as a form of parenting myself, which enabled me to Mother my lad in a more integral way.

Due to the level of tension accumulated, it took around three years for me to actually sense Qi in my hands, and when I did, the curiosity deepened, and another layer of reconnection occurred. I turned to Reiki training to learn how to channel this healing energy and loved how this facilitated an ease for me to treat my boy whenever my hands were holding him. The practice later opened me to my spiritual nature, which showed me how to tune in with his spirit too, connecting higher self to higher self – a mode which reassured me all the way through his teenage years and continues to this day.

As his personality grew stronger, he railed against my healing ways, feigning dis- interest, although he would ask me for Reiki! He once had an experience at a festival where the lass he was with got a bad headache and he soothed it away by placing his hands on her head and basically loving her better.

We can all receive and give healing energy; it's a Love frequency thing and may or may not have a particular name. All you really need is the feeling of Love and a willingness to soften and become a vessel to share the healing Qi.

Qigong shifted how I parent. It's also changed the way I showed up as a daughter, a friend and a partner. Being a witness to my life gave me perspective from where to reflect and respond. This activated a deepening of truer self-care, a nurture I'd longed for, but didn't know where to find. It was always there, waiting for me to return and re-tune. Yes, it's a challenge to keep it up and I still get it wrong sometimes, but the centre is always there gently calling me back.

My Qi practice gave me a place to land that I recognise, a home inside me. The map to find this place comes from engaging with the wisdom of my body, mind, heart and soul. The positive far-reaching effects gave me back to myself and ignited a desire to help others reconnect to their true life-force energy.

In the early years of Qi training, I was still producing costumes and although I'd found ways to heal the impact which that line of work had on my body, I could not see a way through to changing career, until...

The Tao Has Ways of Making You Move

As the turn of the millennium approached, I had been practising Qigong for over five years and had led a few classes, when my teacher was indisposed. This showed me that a new pathway of potential was opening. Creating bespoke wedding dresses had become my art, but it was while completing one made from plush velvet, that intense damage occurred to my forearms, signalling that now was the time to put down my needles and step away from what had become a punishing line of work.

Sharp pains in the thumb nerve and tenosynovitis rendered me unable to use either of my arms AT ALL!! This was a scary 'wake up call to the next level'. How could I take care of my boy properly? I simply could not carry on hurting myself to make money. When I had to go back to wearing the wrist braces from back when the disorder first hit after breastfeeding, I realised I hadn't taken on board enough of the teachings! I can laugh about it now, but at the time I was very anxious.

I had to stop creating the velvet collection immediately.

Thankfully I had a costume-making friend who helped complete the wedding party outfits.

For the next two years, I didn't lift a pin and took to running kids Saturday craft sessions with my lad's mates to encourage their creative play with fabric – I had so much to play with!

I encouraged them to create with colour and form, with simple stitching or tie-dying and fabric painting. It was from these sessions that the Apollo Stars were born, a varying size range of collectible multi-coloured five-pointed star beanie bags and cushions which became an additional way of earning for the first decade of the new millennium.

I broke the abstinence from my sewing machine in the summer of 2000 by making my son a white suit with a silver lining for his 10th birthday party. His theme was Saturday Night Fever, he was channelling his inner John Travolta! We also reformed the space-glam-punk-band for one last appearance in the Stoke Newington Church Street Festival, where my lad wore the white suit and came on to introduce us as Little Jimmy Osmond. What were we like?!

At the time we had no idea that he would become a songwriter and performer, but it turned out that sharing the stage together for this gig was actually a handing over of the 'mic baton', as this was his first appearance fronting a band ...and my last.

Leaving London – Entering the Forest

At this point, we made a decision to move away from London. He was about to start secondary school and I could feel a strong call to be closer to nature. When visiting the New Forest, my connection to the Qi was way easier to sense than in the city. I knew my soul call was drawing us both away into a more supportive place of nurture, in or with Mother Nature – Great GrandMother Earth. I needed this nurture as support for the next phase, Mothering a teenager.

We moved in the late summer of 2000 to a cute thatched cottage, but this later flooded, requiring us to move out swiftly. The friends we knew in the area lived in a cul-de-sac. Lo and behold, a perfect house came up for rent across the road from them. Perfect! We stayed and nurtured our heartful community until my lad turned 18. It was a great support for us all living so close as dear friends, like extended family.

We lived on the edge of a forest enclosure where we could be out the gate and in the forest in a couple of minutes. This was a great boon to our life, our relationship moved into what it needed to be then, quite different from the clear Mother/child one in London. We were in the crazy teenage years, evolving into being friends and family.

Joy! I could do my Qigong practice outside in good weather, feet on the true planet surface, yes!! He would romp around the forest with mates, a great way to let off steam while being held by The Great Mother. Both of us safe in her wise embrace.

With teenage outbursts ramping up, I do recall being triggered by a particular incident, making me run into my treatment room overlooking the meadow. I slammed the door shut to assert my boundary and space, with him ranting on the other side. I began to move the Figure of eight form very fast to express my frustration to invite in balance, and calm.

This is often referred to as the 'Great Harmoniser' in Qigong and it does what it says. As I was swooping through its infinity path either side of my body, the movement slowed its pace and I could feel the balancing directive having an effect in the air around me; or 'the field' as we refer to it. As the calm returned to me, it also had an effect on him.

This was proper magic at play! I have since used this form time and again behind the scenes to invite harmony, and base much of my Qigong and Reiki around this central form.

Becoming 'Home-Free'

My son grew up, and of course eventually moved away from home. This was a layered grieving process for me for sure. He no longer needed me like he used to, and this was a tough adjustment.

Thankfully, I had already nurtured my new career by completing a four year Elemental Qigong teacher training programme, working in three different leisure centres in the New Forest, turning people on to their Qi. This gave me a focus and led me to further training in Reiki, EFT and Colour Psychology. I had the tools to assist me with this massive transformation of our relationship – another lengthening of the apron strings.

There was, however, a downside to making my healing activities my business. I had to work a lot to make enough money to pay the bills. Slowly and surely, I was nearing burnout again and by the time I hit menopause I was done. It was time to Mother myself well, but how?

I knew something had to change. Perhaps if I didn't run a home, I wouldn't need to earn so much and could ditch the toxic relationship I found myself in and let go of most of my work commitments.

Leave home! What??!!

I loved my home and I love sharing my home, so this was a big shift, bringing up another level of bereavement. I reduced my teaching schedule to one weekend a month, vowing to reclaim my personal Qigong practice. This was my Menopause Mumma making me feisty, urging a reclamation to the truth of who I be. Letting go of 'what wasn't me' was key.

As I gave the keys back to the landlord, I knew a huge shift was underway, akin to giving birth to my boy being, all those years ago. I was transitioning from Mother to Crow'ne (as I spell it!), birthing a deeper sense of authentic self.

This became my five year 'Home-Free' period. Thankfully, I had places to live temporarily in Austria, France and Spain, alongside house-sits in the UK. What I hadn't factored in was how my change of circumstance would affect my son.

Massive Shift

When I was out of the country I'd let him drive my car with the agreement that he would deliver me to and collect me from the airport. An arrangement that worked well for us both, giving us also much appreciated in-car time to chat.

On my last visit to Austria to gather the remainder of personal possessions and say goodbye, at last, to a five year relationship, I held back the details of exactly where I was heading due to fear of my son's wrath towards my ex. However, like any suppressed 'secret', it bubbled up, just as we were speeding up the A23 towards Gatwick Airport, with him driving.

He was furious!! How dare I be going back there after blah blah blah...

An old argument, one I had listened to before. Despite the mixture of emotions, I knew his outburst was coming from a fierce sense of protection.

Being yelled at by a steaming son at the wheel of the car speeding full tilt up the motorway scared the life out of me. I reached deep within for guidance, using my Qi centring breath to sink into a deep belly presencing. From here, feeling anchored to Mother Earth through a giant stabilising cord, I trusted that whatever I said next would be a truth he was calling through and ready to hear.

My response was beyond retaliatory defensiveness, rather stoked by a calm breath into my belly and heart saying;

"I hear you."

What followed was a discussion on how people who trigger you are to be thanked because they show you what you are unwilling to see about yourself.

What if his furious reaction was a mirror to him for something else and my triggering of him had become a useful ally?

When his anger initiated me into peace, I knew something profound within our relationship had shifted. It was a significant turning point, one which recurs from time to time, as if testing the waters, or freeing another layer. We became respectful friends from then on. Our Mother/child relationship grew to have added sister/brother overtones! We found a meeting place that gives us somewhere to return to when our views on life sometimes show vast differences of opinion.

Returning and Re-tuning

My lad is my most important 'project' to date. He tries, tests and loves me into finding authentic answers to some of the most important considerations in my life, as I do for him.

He's woken Motherhood up in me in a way I had no idea it could.

As I Mothered him, I learned how to parent myself.

Eventually after living 'away from home' for five years, I found a new place to land in Somerset, but how all that came to be is for another story.

I'm still learning how to foster the most authentic, kind and boundaried relationship I have had in this lifetime.

We are work – and play – in a progressive process.

I realise that I gave birth to a babe, who grew through toddling to schoolboy into a musician and performer of the highest calibre.

He has become my dearest friend and my best brother. He is my sun, and my air.

Qigong gave me a way into healing and meditation to which I would not otherwise have had access. It helps me into a more steady relationship with the Yin Yang dance of life and connection with The Great Mother. When I honour the core principle that every cell of me is seeking balance, levels of calm, peaceful ease that I never knew were possible become me, and nurture me onwards, saging the aging, all being well!

———————————

The spelling of Qi, Chi or Ki depends on the translation used. All refer to the same thing – life-force energy or prana.

Qigong, or Chi Kung are both pronounced 'chee gung' – the cultivation of this life-force energy, using movement, mindset and meditation.

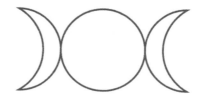

A CHANNELLED MESSAGE FROM MOTHER MARY

By Debra Kilby

I am here, my sweets. I am here all the time, and I am particularly here in this month of May, the month of love, the month of Ma. The Mother in energy. For do you know you are this, even if you are not a Mother or not yet, a Mother is who you are, who we all are birthed from – the Mother, and birthing as the Mother.

And therefore, how can we not hold this energy? This energy has been used as one of separation, who has, who has not, who is, who is not. And yet this energy is healing now, this energy of separation, as you are all to recognise and remember that you are indeed the Mother, just as am I.

For I did not only birth Christ and many other children, I also birthed the light of myself, the light of others, and the birth of a new Dawn. For that is ultimately what I was doing in those times you know me from. And my role has been somewhat amplified, but also restricted as only being known as the Mother of Christ. When in reality, I am the Mother of all Mothers, the Mother of all the Mother Energy that allows for all else to be birthed, whether in person or idea.

And this is the same for you. For you are not only a 'doing' thing as a Mother. And you are not only a separate thing as a Mother. You are a Mother, or not a Mother on the premise of birthing a child. You are a Mother because you are a Mother of all and therefore are able to birth, whatever it is you wish as a Mother.

Do you not Mother your pets, your businesses, your homes, your loved ones in spirit, or here? Do you not Mother the plants you seed or the ideas and inspirations you have? Do you not Mother yourself? For all of this is the Mother, the energy of the Mother, and all it is capable of birthing.

And so in this month of May, we ask you to look at where you Mother, who you Mother and what it means to be a Mother. Not just of your children, but of and as the world. For what you are birthing here is your right.

And your role as Mothers, as creators, as birthers of life and realities that come from a pure sense of the heart and not of the mind. For you can see how the word Mother has impacted the mind and body and all it means, and this is not what it means, Mother. Mother is not what you have or don't have, Mother is not what you are or are not.

Mother is the energy of all of creation. And that may mean birthing the light or not birthing the light, but all is birthing. So I ask you to widen your view on this role and this word for it is time to be known that I am not who you think I am. And neither are you.

For we are so much more than this. So much more than words and identities and haves and have nots. For we are the very creators of life itself. And this is not what they would have you believe about me because it suits their agenda to place the Mother Energy at the back end of the birthing process, and only look at what is birthed and birth, rather than the place and sound, the pinpoint of creation itself.

So do not allow the word Mother to intrude on your thoughts as a point of separation for this is not it at all, this is not you at all. You are the Mother, the birther, the bringer of life and all that this entails.

And so practice this, this month, feeling the energy of the Mother, beyond the word Mother. And feel yourself expand into the heart and truth of it. For it is **now**, you are being asked to birth this energy within and be the Mother.

You already are the Mother of life and to not feel the energy of separation within it, and to not feel the smallness of this word. For I may have once walked small in my human self and body, but I was not small in deed or in action.

And I was not small in how I birthed and seeded the energy of Mother onto this planet, in order for us all to remember the creators and birth as we are, and that we are all capable, more than capable of birthing life itself.

And this is where we are heading – birthing life, is watering the seeds that were planted oh so long ago. And to remember it was not the Mother, let alone the Virgin Mother, who was responsible for the light of Christ and all that transpired. But it was indeed the Mother, the Ma the all that is of the all that is, in the allowing of this light, such as Christ to be birthed.

So turn around your stories of being in the background. Turn around your stories of being the exalted one as the Mother and begin instead to feel and to know the biggest energy of all, is that of Mother, the Ma, the birther of all creations.

And you will see what it is to birth the life and reality you wish to see and be in.

And I am so excited to be with you and open my full heart to you this month. So you can see me not as a person, or a story, or a guide to look up to, but as the energy that allows all, all the above to be birthed, for I am it. And so are you.

And so I ask what it is you would like to birth into the energies of this month? It may well be a child. It may well be yourself. It may well be your idea or your service. But know this, my darlings, it is you, always you, who is the enabler of light, not the other way round.

For it has been said that the Christ will rise again in this lifetime. And my dears, this will transpire. And the reason it will transpire is that you allow it to be so as the Mothers, you are.

I am not leaving the men out of this equation either, for surely they are birthed too through the light of the Mother and therefore are her. However, these creations are very much of the doing variety and often for other reasons than purely birthing light.

And that does not mean they won't get there, for they will. What it does mean is that it is women who can show the way and what it means to be a creator and why. For it is life, you are birthing here.

And that way may well be the birth of a child, but we all know it takes two to tango.

And so my dears also be aware of the balance of the Mother. Just as the masculine has become out of control and we see the consequences of this, so too is the same if there is an imbalance in the feminine.

And even more so if the Ma energy is to become, once again, the dominant force. What is needed here is balance. To honour the creation and the birthing process of them. And then also to be in the mindfulness of how these creations take stock and balance themselves.

Do you see what I mean here my dears? You are all the Mother and birther of life, and yet you are also the balances of life. It is the time of the rise of the Mother God, as Debra puts so eloquently in her book. However, it is also a time of balance and rebalancing the Mother Energy so neither becomes out of control.

There must be balance, there must be respect, and there must be an acknowledgement that all is part of creation. Joseph was my balancer, who is yours? Who is the masculine balancer within you that allows for creation?

The return and rise of the Mother is one which creates fear among many circles. And so it shall be. It is through balance, harmony and understanding of this at play that will ultimately allow for the harmony of the world and indeed the universe.

For all want control of this Mother Energy, but it is not to be controlled. It is to be balanced alongside all the rest, honoured rather than feared, known and felt rather than admired or loathed. Unified rather than separated.

And these are my words for you today with love and heart expansion, as you go into the Mother you already are – in tune and imbalance with all of creation.

And so it is.

Ends.

So just breathing that in. So really feeling this expansion. We can see how the word Mother, and I know the word is really triggering and of course the word is very separating and divisive actually.

So Mary is asking us to expand that we are already, that we are birthed from the Mother, not just our physical Mothers, but from the energy. So she's asking us to look at the energy of Mother, the Ma Energy and how we feel about it. And can we expand into the energy of it?

The bit about Joseph is my balance – I was curious about why she said that because we know relationships come in all forms. But I think it's the masculine within she's talking about. We can see how patriarchy's got completely out of balance and imagine if the Ma energy, the Mother Energy, which I think at some point in time in our millennia probably did, and that would also not be balance. So being aware of the balance within creation.

PART THREE

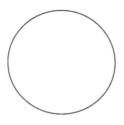

HOW CAN WE
REFRAME MOTHER?

One big part of the collective conversations we enjoyed during the course of creating this book; was there is medicine in sharing our experiences.

Each of us shares a different perspective on Mother.

We wanted to bring to life some of the conversations we enjoyed during our time in circle as a collective of Mothers and we plan to do this through our sacred portal of support and podcasts.

Our reframe of Mother is multi-faceted; but bottom line it came down to this:

- *Mother Energy is in all of us; we are all creators; nurturers and space holders.*

- *To be at our best we need to let go of the 'need' to be perfect and good. There is no right way to Mother. There is only **your** way. And that in itself is perfectly imperfect.*

- *Our children and our businesses often trigger us in response to old wounds. Being conscious of that and noticing why you are feeling upset or angry, is often deep seated in the way we were parented or brought up. Our guidance here is to stop, drop and ground when this comes up for you.*

- *To reframe Mother, it is about connecting with the playful and curious. And taking up space for our own joy, as well as our families. Reconnecting to what you enjoyed as a child is a great way to do this – colouring, writing, drawing, dancing and singing. All the activities that spark creativity can help to connect to that part of you.*

- *To ensure Mother is connected and in community – finding safe spaces to share with no judgment. Many of us in this circle have never met in real life, but met each other on a soul level. Finding a space where you can be unapologetically yourself and begin to fully embody your whole self, is important as you navigate Mother.*

- *Mother is someone who questions, stays grounded and supportive, but understands when it is time to let go; and receive. So much in society has us second guessing what is the right way to do things. It is OK to challenge what we are told to do by authority, family and partners, if it feels off.*

- *Mother witnesses many cycles of birth, death and rebirth. It is our calling to make space to nurture our young and each other through those seasons and cycles, just as the Great Mother holds us each year.*

- *To honour the Great Mother that holds us every minute of every day, giving back to the land that holds us. Being more conscious of our footprints we leave behind. Standing up for our rights. Finding our voices. Together this is how we honour Mother.*

'It takes a village,' isn't just an old saying – it really does take a village or community to bring to life creation IN whatEVER form that takes. If it is a book, a business, a service or a child, seeking circles of support, creating a community that lifts you up, is supportive, nurturing and non-judgemental, however that looks, is essential.

Our community, our collective of Mothers, offer different ways to nurture and support each other through the ebbs and flows of Motherhood.

We would love to share with you some basic practices that can slot easily into your day.

Simple, small steps which will ripple out and gently support you in life as Mother.

We hope you have enjoyed journeying with us and if you wish to continue with us, our Wake Up Mother portal offers resources and wisdom at any stage you find yourself in.

... and the Good Witch of the North summarises it perfectly

"You've always had the power, my dear, you just had to learn it for yourself"

With love.

SUPPORTIVE PRACTICES

Here is just a glimpse of some of the practices some of our authors use to navigate Mother.

Grounding Ritual – The Seasons of Motherhood
By Aimee Strongman

How to connect to the world around you, to help you feel more grounded.

A time of fullness and glow. A woman in full and glorious bloom at the start of the season abundant with heat and energy but within this time we have our own seasonal shifts and cycles, which brings about opportunity to simply be. To reflect upon the wheel of the year to stop and take stock of where we have come and look at where we are going. It's the time to simply be present in the moment and absorb it all.

SUMMER: sizzling, balmy, dreamy, warm, beautiful, fragrant, Sun-kissed, sultry hot and bright.

This is when we are glowing. We are on show. We are in our element in full show, reflecting the sun's rays and beaming in our light. We are here. Ta-da! Exactly where we are supposed to be. Standing tall and proud and looking back at our path. We are at the top of the mountain – we made it, and look at how far we have come. We are in our full moon phase.

WINTER: cool, barren, frosty, slow, dark, spiced, enchanting, crystalline and white.

A time when everything is being turned inwards. This is the moment of the lessons, the nutrients and the guidance of the dark, the shadows and the sense of introspection and personal mist and fog.

This is a hard time of Motherhood when you may feel quite isolated and alone. The days are short, and the nights are long, and it is hard to imagine summer ever existed. But with that uncertainty brings a sense of spaciousness too. Time to read, to bake, to create. To settle down into the hearth, the womb space and tend to your root. The nutrients are returned to make the earth fertile. It is a time for rest.

We are in our dark moon phase.

SPRING: blossoming, blooming, flourishing, green, lively, free, fertile, rejuvenating, colourful, inspiring, awakening, fresh, lively.

Waxing moon bringing the light to us.

This is a time of the new. A new-born self, a blossoming of your inner being and a remembering of the joy this rebirth brings. This is a time of delight and celebration as the light returns and the flowers bloom. A glorious time to plant dream-seeds and wishes for the year ahead to connect with the flora and fauna of the land and to dip into the waters of the Great Mother to cleanse and stir the magic within the wellspring of creation.

AUTUMN: shedding, changing, golden, shifting, earthly, new starts, bountiful, fruitful, vibrant.

This period of change can be felt in our bones. A magnetising shift from light to the darker and the gentle reminder that we are ready to change again. A chance to choose the fruits that are ripe and ready and to make with them what we choose before we begin the journey of introversion. The hunkering and the inward journey we will soon take. The waning moon phase as we sink a little deeper into our depths.

These seasonal moments mirror not just the seasons of the year but our own internal cycles which then connect with our day-to-day Mothering in turn.

We can use them to help assess our feelings and they can serve as a reminder that women are cyclical beings, connected to the moon and her mystical magic. And like our ancestors who used the stars to guide, them so too we can look to nature to show us the way.

Rituals to Keep you Sane
Sarah Lloyd

One thing I found when I became a Mother was it was difficult to carve out time for myself. I increasingly needed to still my mind, because even though we are trying to change this about the world, we still need to exist in it. So please forgive me if you already do these things; but these helped me enormously even when I didn't have children. *And turning to Gin really did not help at all – in fact it just became a sticking plaster to all the issues I wasn't facing! PS. I still enjoy a drink – but that's it – I just enjoy it little and often.*

- Take a Pause – Always give yourself breathing space. When you open your eyes in the morning; when the tempers are flaring. When you don't know the answer to the many questions. Step out and take five. Better yet, explain you are taking five and then do so.

- Connect with your children first thing in the morning; and before they go to bed at night. I know this isn't always possible if you work away. Connecting with them in a loving and nurturing way, even if it's a hug, shows them, they are important to you and sets the day in a positive way.

- Get yourself ready first: This is especially true if you have small kids. I found if I was showered or dressed ready for the day, I always found I could handle whatever came my way.

- Set boundaries: Teach them the importance of body boundaries, behaviour, and space boundaries.

- Play Together: Board games, a good old-fashioned game of catch or kick a ball together. Get involved in their imagination games, just carve out space to play together.

- Talk: Encourage family chats and sharings. Talking about the day after everyone's eaten and decompressed; or just before bed is a lovely way to connect.

- Be there: if your child is struggling with difficult and big emotions; make it known you are there to support them and you love them.

- Find your joy: Being a Mother shouldn't come at a cost to your wellness. Take time out to do things you love. Read a book. Dance. Garden. Sleep. Weekends away. Whatever fills your cup.

These are just a few suggestions that I come back to time and time again. I also highly recommend *Good Inside*; by Dr Becky Kennedy as a great book to support nurturing and supportive parenting practices.

Instant Kidney Chi/Qi activation
By Clara Apollo

As the kidneys are situated in the middle of the back, on either side of the spine, about a third of their tissue nestles into the lungs. By activating our Chi it enables us to connect even further into knowing and ground into Mother.

Try this:

Sitting or standing comfortably drop into the support of the ground beneath you.

Feel the strength of your bones within you and soften into their support.

Let a gentle 'drawing up' occur from the top of your head to the sky, lengthening your spine with ease.

Soften your belly as you breathe, connecting with this power place in you.

Imagine your kidneys as two ear-shaped organs with the top of each nuzzling into the lungs.

As you breathe in, let the energy of the breath travel into your kidneys.

Breathing in a blue hue, breathing out a dusky mist wish is instantly transmuted.

Continue breathing in this way until you sense your kidneys becoming a shiny, deep sapphire blue.

You may like to place your palms over your kidney area on your back and bring in the warmth and connection that way too.

A gentle humming of a soothing tone can complete this process for you..

Tips and Insights from Rachel Haywood

1. Set up support circles before you have your baby – there seems to be a lot of 'pre-birth' support (NCT for example), but everything tends to fall away after the first wee while.

2. When people say it will be hard – ask them to provide solutions! It doesn't prepare me what to feel, prepare me for about what to do for it. People are quite candid about it being hard, but never really explain what that might mean or what might help!

3. It can feel like a Big anti-climax – it feels mean to say that, but I found after all the anticipation (maybe because I'd waited so long to have a baby), the reality didn't always live up to it. And that's OK!

4. Learn the child that you have, not what you prepared for. Really try to know your child and not just whether or not they are measuring up to everyone else.

5. Trust yourself, even when the evidence suggests you were wrong. Don't stop trusting.

6. Leaning away from uncomfortable emotions, means we don't allow the duality of feeling full joy. Lean right in and voice them.

7. Make it stop – I couldn't handle it (the crying/whining?). My nervous system was shot to pieces. It didn't occur to me that sensory overload was a thing for Mums as well as children (or that either of us were neurodivergent). So making time to manage your nervous system is super important for both of you.

8. Thought it was fun, social time with other Mums – but we were all so busy with our babies - so always have non-new Mum friends around! And people who can be around at your house and available to help out. People who know you and can see who you are, even when you are vulnerable and raw and don't feel good in yourself. People who can fetch you back if you're lost and alone and have lost your identity. People who can Mother you.

JOURNALING PROMPTS

We would love to know what comes up for you as you read this book.

We have included some journal prompts in case you would like to explore your own story.

Often the gold we seek is right in front of us all along.

Prompts

- Look in the mirror for a few minutes. As you look at your reflection, pass no judgment. Just notice your unique features and beauty. Describe yourself as a flower, with beauty coming from the inside out.
- Write a love note to yourself.
- Which author's story did you identify with the most?
- Did anything that was shared trigger you? We invite you to explore this... what emotions came up?
- What does Mother mean to you?

- Have you ever considered what your story may look like?
- What makes you unique? How is this freeing?
- What is your heart saying to you today?
- What miracles have you witnessed?
- How do you conquer your fears?
- How do you feel after facing and overcoming your fears?
- When have you been greatly courageous?
- What gratitude fills your heart?
- What would you have done differently?
- Tell of a challenge that you see as a learning experience.
- How do you allow others to support you?
- How can you become more 'wild'?
- To whom would you apologise?

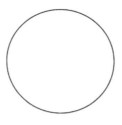

MOTHER...
HOW CAN WE HELP YOU?

Each of our amazing contributors have businesses that support Mothers in some way.

Whether you are an expectant Mother; a Mother of a business. There is a ton of resources available to you.

You can find each of our amazing writers and their offerings on our collective website www.wakeupmother.com

We have also included the bios of our authors should you feel called to reach out directly.

Mother Speaks Radio Show – UK Health Radio

At the time of publishing some of the collaborators of this book where invited to host a podcast and radio show on UK Health Radio. It is here we hope to bring more of these conversations to life and we would love it if you could join us for our regular open, honest Mothers Meeting every week.

Mother Speaks is an unapologetic deep dive, and occasionally stumbling journey into the Mother Energy - from mothering children to businesses, and the wisdom of mother earth herself. This show will share stories and wisdom of Mothers; an opportunity to share real talk, real issues and humor around becoming a mother. Hosted by Clara Apollo, Sarah Lloyd, Zoë Foster and Kathy Bell.

Find us on Substack
https://wakeupmother.substack.com/podcast and Tune in On demand and via https://ukhealthradio.com/listen-on-demand/

Sarah Lloyd

Conscious mother to two little girls, Sarah is passionate about giving those who need one a voice. Through her own brand of magic-based, conscious PR and communications, she has supported many women and entrepreneurial mothers in business to share their stories. She also gets that there is a need to balance it all.

An intuitive, angel communicator and Reiki Energy Master herself, she specialises in working in 'flow' so has thrown the PR rule book out the window. Her mission is to teach and guide changemakers and visionaries to share their stories, without fear, on their terms. Her purpose is to show others it is possible to carve a new way of being.

Her offerings include the Cosmic Connections Container, is a 3 month journey which teaches you how to promote yourself in a way that feels good. Ideal for female entrepreneurs and authors. She supports and holds space as blocks unearthed and transmuted. Opportunities to share and connect outside of the circle are shared, and at the end of the 3 months transformation is guaranteed.

www.indigosoulpr.com / www.sarahlloyd.co

Instagram: sarahlloyd_ispr

Ceryn Rowntree

Ceryn is a Medium, Therapist, Writer and Soul Guide supporting people to remember and re-connect with the deepest power and wisdom of their souls. A practicing witch raised in a family as comfortable working with spirit as with the Earth, Ceryn lives in Northumberland, UK and is the author of two books, The Divine Feminist and The Teen Spirit Guide to Mediumship.

To learn more about Ceryn visit her website at www.cerynrowntree.com or check out her podcasts, The Divine Feminist or Love, Light and Bullshit Bingo.

Kathy Bell

Conscious mother to one, Kathy is an experienced breathwork facilitator, business mentor and published author whose love language is holding loving, clear & expansive spaces for you to ground your soul's essence into your human reality whilst supporting you to step fully into the work that you came here to do.

Kathy has created her own facilitator training to teach others her unique formula for holding safe & sacred spaces and continues to share authentically, from the heart that: "being human is the point" when it comes to spirituality.

Kathy works with conscious leaders, facilitators, coaches and humans who long to be HELD too, so that they can show up radically grounded, spacious and rooted in the truth of The Deepest Connection To Their Souls Purpose

Working 1:1 with Kathy is a sacred space to land as the pressure of life is released, to create the spaciousness inside so there is room to create, show up and live the most authentic Self.

www.kathybell.uk

Instagram: @kathy.bell_

Rachel Haywood

With over 20 years' experience in change and transformation in a project management capacity, Rachel found herself on her own personal change curve that required some course correction.

This included training as a Wayfinding Coach, Rewilding Facilitator and Breathwork Healer to help others chart a course through change and find their most authentic selves on the other side. She is currently writing her story of change with book 'Gardening with Glass (and the magical art of Perseverance)', which details how the shards of glass in the garden of her 1830's home and former pub are a metaphor for the challenges we find in our lives and how they reflect back our true selves and opportunities for growth.

She also runs a support group, Recalibrate, for Mum's with children with additional needs.

To discover how you could work with Rachel, both 1:1 and group options, contact her on rachelbhaywood@gmail.com or check her out on instagram@perseverance_4joy

Katherine Crawley

As founder of AllKatherine, Katherine is a transformational embodiment mentor, drawing on over 30 years of yogic practice, she holds space for high achieving women to shift out of the relentless drive and self-doubt of who they think they should be, to embody the true wisdom and intuitive power of who they truly are, as women.

Guided by her own journey of addiction, being defrauded and the grief of loss, Katherine has been challenged again and again to strip back the layers and go deeper, slowly awakening to the true wisdom and power of her feminine Soul.

With a background in feature-length documentary producing, Katherine has travelled the world, premiered at Sundance and lunched with the stars.

Katherine is trained and experienced in:

- Women's Awakening Coaching
- Yoga Therapy for Women's Health
- Pregnancy Yoga
- Transformational Hatha Yoga
- Sports Yoga Therapy

Published author of *Shakti Farts & Belly Laughs*, out in August 2022 ; Co-producer of award-winning docs, *KZ* and *Black Gold*; Producer and Co-Director of *Fezeka's Voice*, available on Netflix.

Offerings

Women's Yoga – a womb centred practice that aligns you with the wisdom and power of your womanhood. Supports all areas of women's health, as well as fertility, pregnancy, post-natal, perimenopause and menopause. Work one-to-one, join an online class, attend a retreat or purchase the recordings.

All Mother Mentoring – whether you are just embarking on your role as a mother, or already care for one or more children, I am here to support and mentor you to re-connect to the power and wisdom of your womanhood. Whether you are physically exhausted, emotionally overwrought or mentally stressed and strained, know that there is a way through.

You are not alone and within you, you hold all the intuitive wisdom you need to embrace and reclaim this time in your life.

All Katherine workshops & talks – empowering women within the workplace to reconnect to the power and wisdom of their womanhood and step into their true authentic leadership. The children, the Earth, our communities and our hearts need women to remember the essence of who they truly are.

A powerful offering for any day of the month and especially International Women's Day.

To organise a discovery call, please reach out to me at;
allkatherine1111@gmail.com
www.allkatherine.com

Aimee Strongman

Aimee is a lightworker and modern mystic holding space holistically with the Goddesses from Maiden to Mother. She is passionate about supporting women during all the seasons of womanhood in particular during pregnancy and motherhood. Aimee offers practical and positive advice encouraging you to meet with your Inner Goddess at this sacred time of creation.

Working intuitively with the elements and nature, Aimee uses Yoga, somatics, biomechanics, ritual and healing to support women during pre-conception, pregnancy, birth and beyond. This soul-led guidance is at the heart of her unique offerings and her vision is to serve women with love, so they can reconnect with their power, at this sacred time of creation.

Aimee is a Mother to two boys, both born at home, her sun and moon. She is Keeper of the Hearth, a Yoga teacher, Birth-keeper and lives in Dorset. She is the founder of Gather and Glow, and works both online and in person. She offers bespoke sessions, Women's Circles and hosts the Ten Moons Motherhood Retreats. These take place throughout the wheel of the year, complimented by her wild makes from her home lands of Dorset and Avalon @four_winds_wild_makes.

BA Hons, PGCE, Level 4 Accredited BWY Teacher, Pre and Postnatal Yoga Teacher. Featured in Vogue and Stylist Magazine.
Please reach out for a chemistry call to see how we may weave together at this precious time. It would be wonderful to connect.
aimee@gatherandglow.co.uk
www.gatherandglow.co.uk
@glowyoga_studio

Emma While

A mother, early years & adult learning specialist, positive psychology geek, lover of squirrels, wild swimmer, NLP practitioner, mindfulness teacher, writer and owner of *Courage & Chamomile* (purveyors of transformational coaching for mothers since 2016).

Since breaking free from her own suffocating little cage (of society's expectations of her as well as those she had foisted upon herself), Emma has been passionate about empowering other mums to do the same...

... to believe in and BECOME their full, unapologetic selves, beyond the identity of 'mum' or any other roles they play. To let go of the shame, the guilt, the rules, the shoulds and the shouldn'ts, the I can'ts and I have tos. To break the cycles and the patterns, to consciously curate the passionate, exciting and fulfilling life they both desire and deserve, and dream into being a future fit for the next generation we're raising.

Because right now, this world needs a change, and Emma believes that fully empowered, impassioned mothers are the ones to lead it. It's her mission to create a paradigm shift in the way the world views and values mothers and motherhood, and it starts by guiding other mothers to shift the way they feel about themSELVES.

So if you've forgotten who you really are and are ready to become part of this change, ready to remembHer your way back to who you were before the world got to you, reach out to find out more about Emma's 1:1 and group coaching programs, and the ReWilding Motherhood Facilitator Certification to train to do this work for yourself and spread the magic even further!

hello@courageandchamomile.com
Instagram @courageandchamomile
Facebook/Groups/rewildingmotherhood

Dulcie Batt

Founder of JoyFULL Mamas and creator of the Empowered Birth Digital Programme

Dulcie is Mama of 4 children, Founder of JoyFULL Mamas and creator of the online Empowered Birth Programme. Helping women remember their POWER in pregnancy, birth and beyond.

If you are pregnant and wish to feel more calm, comfort & confidence, then connect with her for: Pregnancy Yoga; Hypnobirthing Power Group courses and 1:2:1s; Flourish Pregnancy Retreat Days; and the online digital Empowered Birth Programme.

Then once your baby has landed earthside - she is there as your guide through the first year of Matrescence with Mama & Baby yoga, Mama Workshops and Flourish Mama Retreat Days. Sprinkling joy on your experience throughout!

All of her work as an NLP Coach, Yogi, Qoya teacher & Birthing Hypnotherapist guides women towards their body's incredible innate wisdom and cultivates a deep sense of self trust. The education and inspiration means they enjoy their pregnancy more, with mind, body & soul alignment & grow in confidence each day through birth and beyond. Her dear wish is for Mamas to feel GOOD on this gift of a Mamahood journey!

So if you are pregnant, or a new Mama, Dulcie invites you to connect & is so excited to be your guide. The JoyFull Mamas website has details of all her offerings & information to connect for a free 15 minute consultation.

Dulcie is registered with FEDANT (Federation of Antenatal Educators)
https://www.joyfullmamas.com
www.instagram.com/joyfulmammas
https://www.facebook.com/joyfullmamas

Alison Cooper

Alison is a channel and weaver of energy within Universal laws.

She assists people in healing and remembering all that they are by using sound, including light language, holding space and mentoring in a non judgemental way. In addition to one to one and group sessions, Alison channels artwork, works with energies within buildings and the land for our Divine Mother Gaia.
https://www.alisoncooper.net
https://www.amazon.co.uk/Over-Rainbow-Miscarriage-Baby-Journal

Carrie J Myers

Based in the US, Carrie is a yoga instructor and former studio owner, poet and program developer. She also has a Master of Social Work degree from UNC - Chapel Hill. Carrie is a native of Asheville NC, mother of three, and has been writing since she was 10 years old.

Most of her work is poetry which reflects the phases of her life and helped her process her journey along the way. As a yoga instructor, she discovered new ways to dig deep into her subconscious, pulling from her practice, the words that held higher meaning and growth. As she puts her work out into the world, she hopes to inspire change in the hearts and souls of her readers, while holding space for each interpretation to resonate with each soul's purpose. Carrie is passionate about creating and recognising the beauty in the mess that life can throw at us, at times. Her goal is to help readers to rediscover their authentic selves and revive, create and discover their light within. Her passion is people, inspiring them, loving them and helping them heal from traumas.

www.Carriemyersauthor.com
www.yourselfprogram.com
Instagram@cjmyerspoet @cj_hotyoga @yourselfprogram

Zoë K. M. Foster

Zoë channels immersive, energy art as mega-manifestation portals for divinely feminine rebels. She is also the creator of her SacredExpression™ method, combining sacred geometry, Jungian mandala psychology and fully-embodied, energy-expanding self-expression.

Into her work, she brings over 20 years of training and experience as a cognitive psychologist, yoga teacher, energy worker, and spiritually-creative misfit.

From her barn studio space in the wilds of mid-Devon, she hosts energy-shifting women's circles, messy art workshops and energy-art open days.

Find out more about the SacredExpression™ Method (zoekmfoster.com/sacredexpressiontm) and how it invites you to play, and to really trust the wisdom of the body and all her energies – *child, maiden, mother, crone, and divine.* In this sacred space, we cannot help but begin the journey of inhabiting and expanding into our most fully expressed selves – with utmost integrity.

Behind the Paint - Get intimate with Zoë in her studio where the immersive energy art happens! Be the first to discover what she is painting, what her current inspirations and challenges are, and have your say on her creative decisions! DM her for an invite!

Cosmic Transmissions Incoming (zoekmfoster.substack.com) Juicy, curious, and often provocative content that does not fit into the mainstream social media model. Read, discuss, and give your feedback within the community, and don't forget to read the series where she shares her 'My Failed Book' story (and how it led to her completely unbound book, *It's Written in the Stars: Poems, Reflections & Transmutations on Becoming!*).

Zoë writes regularly for the mainstream and spiritual press, and co-hosts 'Mother Speaks' on UK Health Radio, YouTube and Podcast.

zoekmfoster.com
IG/FB/Twitter @zoekmfoster

Jennifer Flint

Jennifer Flint is a leadership coach, mentor, independent celebrant, and speaker. A Master NLP Practitioner and qualified coach, she is a passionate writer and recently published her first novel, *Wild Egg: A story of one woman's search for her childfree life.* It's for women who are questioning whether Motherhood is their path, and those searching for a deeper experience of being alive, beyond the role of being a Mother.

She lives by the seaside in the North-East of England with her dog, Pip. She enjoys spending free time in her off-grid cabin in Northumberland.

Email: wildegg22@gmail.com
Instagram: https://www.instagram.com/wildegg21/
Facebook: https://www.facebook.com/JenEFlint
Wild Egg - https://www.amazon.co.uk/Wild-Egg-womans-search-childfree/

Clara Apollo

Clara is an Elemental Qigong and Meditation tutor, personal energy mentor, broadcaster, writer and Mum-of-One. She encourages you to tune in, turn on and drop in to your Qi - vital life-force energy - for a well-balanced, healthy and empowered life.

Along with her love of Qi energy play, Clara includes Reiki, FreeMind Hypnotherapy, Sound Healing, Shamanic Practices, Ecstatic Dance, and Colour Psychology to help create a grounded, intuitive space for you to access, express and nurture your unique wellbeing needs.

An ex-nurse and costume designer, Clara became an Elemental Qigong teacher and Usui Reiki Master after a severe RSI on her forearms made it impossible to continue her previous career. After her son left home, so did she - living 'HomeFree' for 5 years exploring Europe, creating Qigong retreats, producing radio shows and running the UK based Conscious Living Events. Life on the road eventually ran its course and she heeded the call to rehome herself, on the lands of Avalon, Somerset.

Clara offers online and in person Qigong sessions, teacher training, 1:1 and retreats, adding 'Free Your Qi' Inner Alchemy hypno-meditation journeys when called to deepen into your multidimensional presence.

Clara hosts 'Chi Time' and 'Mother Speaks' on UK Health Radio, YouTube and Podcast and was awarded 'Media Excellence of the Year 2022' from the 22nd World Congress of Qigong/Tai Chi/TCM/Natural Healing.

https://claraapollo.com
Apollo Qi App https://apolloqi.passion.io
YT https://www.youtube.com/user/chitimetv/
Pod https://spoti.fi/3ntoaUm
IG @clarajoapollo

Debra Kilby

A mother of two boys and 5 babies in spirit. Debra is an energy healer, channel, spirit baby medium and author of Rosa's Choice: Healing the wounds of the mother.

It was through her own challenging journey to motherhood through miscarriage and termination for medical reasons that she awakened to a much bigger picture of life before life – the preparations and choices we made before coming to earth, why we chose to come and the experiences we wished to have.

Understanding life in the here and now – what we're here for, our role and gifts. And also life after death and how we can still connect with our babies and loved ones.

Debra's role in this lifetime is to support women to remember who they are, their value and power meeting their ancient and new to gain a deeper understanding of themselves, birth more of who they are and their own truth, open up their natural intuitive gifts and power and if in conception, birth their babies.

Debra runs a spiritual fertility hub with events throughout the year at Fire + Alchemy in Shoreditch, London. Fire + Alchemy | Crystals (fireandalchemy.com)

She offers one to one support for women who are struggling to conceive, have experienced baby loss or a traumatic birth, they're own or their children's.

www.debrakilby.com
https://www.amazon.co.uk/Rosas-Choice-journey-spirit-together

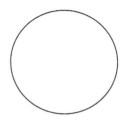

GRATITUDE

Thank you for journeying with us.

We are grateful you have this book in your hand and felt called to read our stories and sample this medicine.

May you go on to share with other Mothers who you feel need to read our stories or hear yours.

Huge gratitude to all the authors who contributed to this project. It would not be possible without you, and thank you for hearing the call.

Thank you to Nicola Humber and the Unbound Press crew – for holding our space, whilst we wove and spun.

Thank you for the Shakti Farters for your love, support and encouragement.

Thank you. Thank you. Thank you.

And so it is.

FURTHER RESOURCES

As we are storytellers, we would be remiss if we didn't share the books and resources we have found useful in our own journeys and these can be found at all good book shops.

What Mothers Do – Naomi Stadlen
How Mothers Love – Naomi Stadlen
Good Inside – Dr Becky Kennedy
Why Did No-One Tell Me – Emma Brockwell
Mothers Talking – Active Birth Centre
Wild Egg – Jennifer Flint
Unbound – Nicola Humber
Shakti Farts and Belly Laughs – The Unbound Press
Real Birth: Women Share their Stories – Robin Green
My Wild Sleepless Nights – Clover Stroud
Daring Greatly – Brené Brown
The Gifts of Imperfect Parenting – Brené Brown
Mother Pukka – The Portal for those Who Happen to be Parents
Untamed – Glennon Doyle

Other Useful Numbers to Contact if You are Struggling

Home Start: Help for families and young children through challenging times.
https://www.home-start.org.uk

PANDAS: Help for Mothers with PND
Tel: 0808 1961 776
https://pandasfoundation.org.uk

My Sisters House: Support for women
Tel: 01243 697800
https://www.mysistershouse.info

Cruse: Bereavement Support for families
Tel: 0808 808 1677
https://www.cruse.org.uk

Wellbeing of Women: Save and change the lives of women, girls and babies, through research, education and advocacy
hello@wellbeingofwomen.org.uk
https://www.wellbeingofwomen.org.uk/

Lightning Source UK Ltd.
Milton Keynes UK
UKHW022034030223
416446UK00011B/882